Critical Acclaim For Books By Gen & Kelly Tanabe

Authors of *Get Into Any College, Get Free Cash For College* and *Accepted! 50 Successful College Admission Essays*

"Upbeat, well-organized and engaging, this comprehensive tool is an exceptional investment for the college-bound."

—Publishers Weekly

"What's even better than all the top-notch tips is that the book is written in a cool, conversational way."

—College Bound Magazine

"A 'must' for any prospective college student."

—Midwest Book Review

"Invaluabl m the elimination of admission scholarship funds."

nard Banks, *The Journal Press*

"A present

tz, *The Honolulu Advertiser*

"Helpful, well ies of act etters and essays and pre for all st ts."

—KLIATT

"When you consider the costs of a four-year college or university education nowadays, think about forking out (the price) for this little gem written and produced by two who know."

—Don Denevi, Palo Alto Daily News

"The Tanabes literally wrote the book on the topic."

—Bull & Bear Financial Report

MONEY-WINNING SCHOLARSHIP ESSAYS AND INTERVIEWS

You can win or lose a scholarship by your essay or interview. This book shows you how to win.

Step-by-step instructions on how to craft a winning essay and ace any interview.

Read 30 money-winning essays.

Meet students who won $3 million in scholarships.

Designed to help high school and college students.

Gen S. Tanabe ▪ Kelly Y. Tanabe

Harvard graduates and award-winning authors of the books
Get Into Any College ▪ *Get Free Cash For College*
Accepted! 50 Successful College Admission Essays

Special contributions by Gregory James Yee

Money-Winning Scholarship Essays And Interviews
By Gen S. Tanabe and Kelly Y. Tanabe

Published by SuperCollege, LLC
4546 B10 El Camino Real, #281
Los Altos, CA 94022
650-618-2221
www.supercollege.com

Credits: Cover design by TLC Graphics. Edited by Bob Drews. All essays in this book are used by permission of their authors.

Trademarks: All brand names, product names and services used in this book are trademarks, registered trademarks or tradenames of their respective holders. SuperCollege is not associated with any college, university, product or vendor.

Disclaimers: The authors and publisher have used their best efforts in preparing this book. It is intended to provide helpful and informative material on the subject matter. Some narratives and names have been modified for illustrative purposes. SuperCollege and the authors make no representations or warranties with respect to the accuracy or completeness of the contents of the book and specifically disclaim any implied warranties or merchantability or fitness for a particular purpose. There are no warranties which extend beyond the descriptions contained in this paragraph. The accuracy and completeness of the information provided herein and the opinions stated herein are not guaranteed or warranted to produce any particular results. SuperCollege and the authors specifically disclaim any responsibility for any liability, loss or risk, personal or otherwise, which is incurred as a consequence, directly or indirectly, of the use and application of any of the contents of this book.

ISBN 0-9657556-1-4

Manufactured in the United States of America
10 9 8 7 6 5 4 3 2 1

Cataloging-in-Publication Data
Gen S. Tanabe, Kelly Y. Tanabe
    Money-Winning Scholarship Essays And Interviews / by Gen S. Tanabe and Kelly Y. Tanabe. —1st ed.
            p.   cm.
    Includes appendices and index.
    ISBN 0-9657556-1-4
    1. College Guides   I. Title
    2. Reference   3. Personal Finance

CONTENTS AT A GLANCE

1   The Secret To Winning A Scholarship / 13

2   How To Find Great Scholarships / 19

3   Judges' Roundtable: Inside The Selection Process / 29

4   How To Write A Money-Winning Essay / 45

5   30 Money-Winning Essays / 63

6   12 Essays That Bombed / 129

7   Judges' Roundtable: The Scholarship Essay / 151

8   Winning Interview Strategies / 159

9   Interview Question & Answer Examples / 175

10   Judges' Roundtable: The Interview / 203

11   Final Thoughts / 211

Appendix A: Scholarship Directory / 215

Appendix B: Web Guide / 239

Index / 243

TABLE OF CONTENTS

Chapter 1. The Secret To Winning A Scholarship / 13

You are 60 seconds away from the trash bin / 14
The scholarship strategies you'll learn / 15
Why we know so much about scholarships / 16
Not just looking for straight "A" students / 17

Chapter 2. How To Find Great Scholarships / 19

Scholarship goldmines / 20
Looking to make an impact / 21
Ambassadors wanted / 23
Which scholarship is right for you? / 24
Work experience & financial aid / 25
Their mission is your mission / 26
When & where to find scholarships / 27
Inside information from past winners / 27

Chapter 3. Judges' Roundtable: Inside The Selection Process / 29

Meet your scholarship judges / 30
What is the purpose of your award? / 30
Who typically judges the scholarship competition? / 32
How does your scholarship selection process work? / 34
What qualities do you look for when selecting the winner? / 36
What sets the winner apart from the runner-up? / 39
What advice do you have for future applicants? / 40
Participating judges & experts / 42

Chapter 4. How To Write A Money-Winning Essay / 45

Why the essay is critical to winning / 46
Focus on solutions / 47
The making of a powerful essay / 47
Three common features of all money-winning essays / 49
Hard to believe but true essay mistakes / 51
How to find the perfect topic / 53
Essay writing tips / 53
    Remember to focus on originality / 53

Share something personal / 54
Test your thesis with a simple question / 54
Expand on your accomplishments / 56
Beware of meaningless facts / 56
Don't write a sob story / 56
Show some positive energy / 58
The importance of going beyond the superficial / 55
An essay pop quiz / 57
The importance of editors / 58
Use examples & illustrate / 59
Recycle & reuse / 59
How to write a great introduction & conclusion / 60
Essays get better with each revision / 61

Chapter 5. 30 Money-Winning Essays / 63

The money-winning essays / 64
Experiences & challenges / 65
A scholarship support network / 69
The intangible benefits of applying / 75
Essays about family / 76
National or international issues / 84
Essay advice from the winners / 85
The importance of getting editors / 96
Community service & volunteerism / 97
Career plans or fields of study / 103
Essays about leadership / 112
Academic accomplishments / 114
More essay advice from the winners / 119
Essays about athletics / 120
Artistic talents / 122
A parent's essay / 125
Seeking genuineness / 127

Chapter 6. 12 Essays That Bombed / 129

Learning from failure / 130
Where's the point? / 130
The attempted tearjerker / 132
Miss America essay / 133
The life-changing voyage / 135
Convoluted vocabulary / 137
Behold! My statistics / 138

The most influential person in the world / 139
Be true / 141
Creativity overload / 141
The future me / 143
My life as seen on TV / 144
Excuses, excuses, excuses / 146
Complex problem, simple solution / 148

Chapter 7. Judges' Roundtable: The Scholarship Essay / 151

Meet your scholarship judges / 152
How important is the essay to winning a scholarship? / 152
What qualities make an essay powerful? / 152
What common mistakes do students make on the essay? / 154
Participating judges & experts / 157

Chapter 8. Winning Interview Strategies / 159

Face-to-face with the interview / 160
Two types of interviews / 160
How to ace your interview—friendly or hostile / 161
Transform an interrogation into a conversation / 161
Advice from a Rhodes Scholar / 163
You are not the center of the universe / 164
Dress & act the part / 165
The group interview / 165
What it's like to be an interviewer / 167
How to make practice into perfect / 168
The long-distance interview / 169
The hostile interview / 170
The disaster interview / 171
Post-interview / 172
Make sure you make your point / 173

Chapter 9. Interview Question & Answer Examples / 175

Giving the right answers / 176
Achievements & leadership questions / 176
Tip #1 from a scholarship winner / 179
Personal questions / 179
Misinterpreting the judges / 181
Why you deserve to win questions / 184
Education & college questions / 186
Tip #2 from a scholarship winner / 187

Academic questions / 189
Tip #3 from a scholarship winner / 191
Your career & future questions / 194
Tip #4 from a scholarship winner / 195
Activity questions / 198
Opinion questions / 200
Tip #5 from a scholarship winner / 201

Chapter 10. Judges' Roundtable: The Interview / 203

Meet your scholarship judges / 204
How important is the interview in determining who wins? / 204
What are some typical questions that you ask? / 205
What are qualities of a good interview? / 206
What common mistakes do students make in interviews? / 207
How should students prepare for interviews? / 208
Participating judges & experts / 210

Chapter 11. Final Thoughts / 211

A personal ending / 212
Special request / 213

Appendix A: Scholarship Directory / 215

A directory of select awards and scholarships that appear in this book including information on how to apply.

Appendix B: Web Resources / 239

The best resources on the Internet to help you with scholarships and financial aid.

Index / 243

SPECIAL FEATURES

Stories & Advice From Winners & Judges

These stories of success and failure from students and advice from judges and experts are both entertaining and enlightening.

Not just looking for straight "A" students / 17
Looking to make an impact / 21
Ambassadors wanted / 23
Work experience & financial aid / 25
When & where to find scholarships / 27
Focus on solutions / 47
Hard to believe but true essay mistakes / 51
The importance of going beyond the superficial / 55
An essay pop quiz / 57
Use examples & illustrate / 59
Essays get better with each revision / 61
A scholarship support network / 69
The intangible benefits of applying / 75
Essay advice from the winners / 85
The importance of getting editors / 96
More essay advice from the winners / 119
Seeking genuineness / 127
Be true / 141
Advice from a Rhodes Scholar / 163
The group interview / 165
What it's like to be an interviewer / 167
The hostile interview / 170
Make sure you make your point / 173
Tip #1 from a scholarship winner / 179
Misinterpreting the judges / 181
Tip #2 from a scholarship winner / 187
Tip #3 from a scholarship winner / 191
Tip #4 from a scholarship winner / 195
Tip #5 from a scholarship winner / 201

Judges' Roundtable: Chapters 3 - 7 - 10

We sat down with judges and experts from around the country to find out what it takes to win a scholarship. Read their frank advice on what students have done right and wrong.

This book would not have been possible without the selfless contributions of scholarship winners, judges and experts. They gave their time and shared their knowledge for your benefit.

We would like to recognize the special contributions made by Gregory James Yee.

We dedicate this book to all of the people who helped to make it possible. And to you, our dear reader, we hope you will use these lessons to create your own money-winning scholarship essays and interviews.

CHAPTER ONE

THE SECRET TO WINNING A SCHOLARSHIP

In this chapter:

■ Why you are 60 seconds away from the trash bin

■ How your essay or interview will make or break your chances of winning a scholarship

■ Why you can win even without straight "A's"

■ Who we are and why we know so much about winning scholarships

You Are 60 Seconds Away From The Trash Bin

If you witnessed the judging of a scholarship competition, you'd be surprised at how quickly decisions are made. It's not unusual for scholarship judges to conclude in less than 60 seconds whether your application advances to the next round or gets tossed into the rejection pile.

What's the secret to capturing the attention of these discriminating judges and dramatically improving your chances of winning? For most scholarships the secret is in your **essay** or **interview**. These give the judges the insight they need to separate the winners from the runner-ups.

If you are like the majority of scholarship applicants you aren't sure what makes a winning essay or interview. And why should you be? It's unlikely that you have access to dozens of past scholarship winners who can share their experiences and open up their winning essays and interview answers for examination.

And it is even more unlikely that you have interviewed scholarship judges and experts who can tell you exactly what qualities they look for when selecting a winner. Obviously, anyone with this kind of access and knowledge has a tremendous advantage.

Now you do.

In this book you will meet past scholarship winners, read their essays and interviews and learn the strategies that they have used to win $3 million in awards. (That amount is not a misprint. In fact, one incredible student won over $1 million in scholarship offers!) You will also have total access to scholarship judges who will take you inside the selection process to reveal what they look for when choosing winners.

Unlike any other scholarship book, in this book you will learn how to:

Find the scholarships that you are most likely to win. We identify the best places to find awards and strategies for selecting those that are your best prospects.

Craft a money-winning scholarship essay. We believe that the best way to learn how to win is from the experiences of others. In this book we show you 30 actual scholarship essays that were used by students like you to win money. Our complete essay-writing workshop guides you step-by-step through selecting a topic, writing and editing your own money-winning scholarship essay.

Avoid costly essay mistakes. Failure can be the best teacher. Through 12 essays that bombed, you will see exactly how to prevent the mistakes that have doomed others.

Interview confidently and skillfully. With comprehensive interview strategies and examples of over 20 questions you are likely to be asked along with successful answers, you will have everything you need to ace scholarship interviews.

Understand what scholarship judges want. The Judges' Roundtables pinpoint what scholarship judges seek in selecting the winners. This select group of experts has seen thousands of applications and decided the fate of many applicants. Their lessons and advice are indispensable.

Remember that you have a limited amount of time to make your mark in the scholarship selection process. With this book, you can learn how to make your 60 seconds count.

The Scholarship Strategies You'll Learn

Here is what you will learn in each chapter:

Chapter 2: How To Find Great Scholarships. There are a lot of scholarships available, but the first step to success is to know where to look and how to select the awards that you have the best chance of winning.

Chapter 3: Judges' Roundtable: Inside The Selection Process. Meet actual judges and understand from their perspective what it takes to win scholarships.

Chapter 4: How To Write A Money-Winning Essay. In this information-packed chapter we give you everything you need to craft a powerful essay. We guide you step-by-step from selecting a topic to using effective writing techniques to avoiding common mistakes.

Chapter 5: 30 Money-Winning Essays. See how strategy is put into action in these real essays that won $3 million in scholarships. See how your essay compares and be inspired by these successes.

Chapter 6: 12 Essays That Bombed. The best lessons often come from failure—and preferably the failure of someone else! We have 12 disaster essays that didn't win. Each illustrates an important lesson of what not to do in your essay.

Chapter 7: Judges' Roundtable: The Scholarship Essay. Many of the scholarship judges have read hundreds if not thousands of essays and know what works and what doesn't. See for yourself what the judges have to say about the making of a winning essay.

Chapter 8: Winning Interview Strategies. Learn how to deliver a knockout interview. Discover what every good interviewee knows and how to overcome interview stage fright.

Chapter 9: Interview Question & Answer Examples. Preview typical interview questions and review example responses to learn what makes a powerful answer.

Chapter 10: Judges' Roundtable: The Interview. Find out what the judges are really listening for when they interview you.

Chapter 11: Final Thoughts. Our final tips and thoughts before you embark on your journey to mastering money-winning essays and interviews.

Why We Know So Much About Scholarships

You may be wondering who we are and what we know about winning scholarships. As the authors of three other books on college admission and scholarships, *Get Into Any College, Get Free Cash For College* and *Accepted! 50 Successful College Admission Essays,* we have had the unusual opportunity to meet thousands of stu-

Not Just Looking For Straight "A" Students
Discover Card Tribute Award Scholarship

You might think that scholarships seek only students with perfect SAT scores and flawless GPAs. This is not true. Many scholarships including those awarded by Discover® Card are looking beyond grades and test scores.

For the Discover Card Tribute Award® Scholarship, the judges look at many factors besides grades, and test scores are not even requested in the application.

"We believe that success in life is more than a GPA. It's also what you can accomplish in your personal life and in your community," says Shirley Kennedy Keller, program director of the American Association of School Administrators, which administers the Tribute Award.

Keller encourages all students to apply, even those with less than perfect academic records or test scores. "This scholarship applies to virtually every high school junior who has a B minus to C plus grade point average who wants to continue their education or training beyond high school. That hopefully provides some encouragement to students who say that scholarships don't apply to me," she says.

The message is clear: If you don't have perfect grades or test scores don't let that prevent you from applying for awards.

dents and scholarship judges. In writing this book we conducted extensive research and interviewed dozens of scholarship judges and scholarship-winning students.

But perhaps more important than this research is the fact that we've been where you are today. Both before and during college we were fanatical about applying for scholarships. Using the strategies that we have incorporated into this book we won over $100,000 in merit-based scholarships. This went a long way in helping us to leave Harvard debt-free and our parents guilt-free.

In addition, we have served as scholarship judges. In particular, one scholarship that we judge is the SuperCollege.com Scholarship, which receives over 10,000 applications each year. Reading these application essays, we have seen what works as well as what mistakes students make over and over. We are also expert interviewers, having conducted both scholarship interviews and admission interviews for Harvard.

The sum total of this experience, research and know-how is contained within these pages. If you follow these strategies you too can become a scholarship winner. Remember that someone is going to win each award. We want to help make that someone be you.

CHAPTER TWO

HOW TO FIND GREAT SCHOLARSHIPS

In this chapter:

■ Scholarship goldmines

■ How to decide which scholarships to apply to and which to avoid

■ How to uncover the mission of any scholarship

Scholarship Goldmines

When we were searching for scholarships, we found them in nearly every place imaginable. Some we discovered in the dusty collection of books at our library. Others by serendipitous newspaper announcements of past winners. We even found an award advertised on a supermarket shopping bag.

Having personally spent hundreds of hours scouring the planet for scholarships and meeting dozens of other successful scholarship winners, we have learned where most scholarships are hidden. To help make your scholarship hunt more efficient, we present what we believe are the best places to look.

As you search, keep in mind that not every scholarship you find is one you should apply for. As your list of possibilities grows you need to evaluate each award to determine if it is right for you. Don't worry—we'll show you how to do this later in the chapter. But knowing which awards to pass on is vital in allowing you to focus your time and energy on those awards that you have the best chance of winning.

The first two obvious places to find scholarships are:

Books. There are a number of scholarship directories from which to choose. When looking for a guide, seek one that offers descriptions of the awards, including deadlines and contact information. Most importantly, make sure that the book has an easy-to-use index. You don't have time to read through every scholarship listed so an index will help narrow down your choices quickly. For example, our scholarship guide, *Get Free Cash For College*, not only contains hundreds of awards worth over $1.1 billion, but also has 21 different indexes based on criteria like field of study, state of residence, ethnicity, athletics, organization affiliation, hobbies, talents and much more to help you pick the best awards.

Internet Databases. A great way to find scholarships for free is through the Internet. One of the benefits of online scholarship directories is that they can be updated often. Thus, if you search an online scholarship directory you will usually find up-to-date information on the newest scholarships. Check out the free schol-

Looking To Make An Impact
Tyco Capital is Pro Education Program

The overriding goal of the Tyco Capital is Pro Education program is to have the greatest impact. The program is sponsored by the New Jersey-based financial services company and provides awards worth over $40,000 and internship opportunities to students from 10 inner-city high schools in Newark each year.

"We don't give the award to the valedictorian. We give where we feel our award will make the biggest impact," says Janet L. Horowitz, assistant vice president of corporate philanthropy.

Horowitz says that what sets the winners apart from the finalists is that the students demonstrate confidence, leadership and a desire to make a difference.

Underscoring the mission of the award, Tyco Capital requires that winners also agree to volunteer in their community. The recipients must log over 20 hours for each year that they earn the award. Tyco Capital even assists the students in finding places to volunteer.

arship search on our website at www.supercollege.com. By creating a personal profile you can let our database do the work of finding awards that match you.

While scholarship books and online databases are popular methods for finding scholarships, you also need to look beyond them since no single directory can list every scholarship available.

We believe that one of the best places to find scholarships is right in your own backyard—your community.

Counselor or financial aid officer. Do this right now. Call your counselor or financial aid officer and make an appointment. Before the meeting, understand how much money you need for college and prepare a resume or list of your activities and awards. During the meeting explain your situation and ask if there are any scholarships that your counselor or advisor can recommend.

These counselors and financial aid officers probably know more about the awards available in your community and on campus than anyone else.

It's important whenever you speak to a counselor (either in high school or college) that you inquire about any scholarships that require a nomination. With these competitions, the applicant pool is almost always smaller. The most difficult hurdle is that you need to get nominated. You have nothing to lose by asking, and if nothing else, it shows how serious you are about financing your education.

Activities. Many clubs and organizations on campus offer awards for their members. You should check with the officers or advisors to see what is available. Also check with the booster organizations, if your group has one, since they may also provide scholarship funds.

Professional organizations. For practically every career field there exists one or more professional organization. These groups often offer awards for students in their field. For example, the American Marketing Association provides information about awards for those studying marketing.

Community organizations. You don't have to belong to an organization to win. In fact, many community groups raise money with the intent of giving it away to members of their community. Local Rotary and Lions clubs often offer scholarships for outstanding students in the community whether or not their parents are members. They view their scholarship programs as part of their service to the community. Open a phone book or go online and call the 10 largest organizations in your area.

Employer. If you have a full- or part-time job, check with your employer for awards. Many companies offer educational support as an employee benefit. If your employer doesn't offer a scholarship, suggest that they start one.

Parents' employer. Companies often award scholarships to the children of their employees. Ask your parents to speak with their human resources department about scholarships and other educational programs offered to employees and their families.

Ambassadors Wanted
Rotary International Ambassadorial Scholarships

Designed to promote international understanding, the Ambassadorial Scholarships program has assisted over 30,000 men and women from 100 nations since the program began in 1947.

"We're looking for the people who want to give something back to the community, people who we hope will make a difference in the world," says Russ Hobbs, a district scholarship chairman in the San Francisco Bay Area. "We're not looking for someone who will go back to their community or company and not give anything back."

Previous recipients in Hobbs' district have included an aspiring politician who speaks five languages, a former teacher who has interned with the United Nations and the holder of a patent for a shallow water pump.

One of the reasons why recipients of the Rotary award must be committed to making a difference is that they are ambassadors representing their home country abroad. As a part of the program, scholars make presentations about their home country in the countries in which they study. Brent Drage of Rotary International says that the organization seeks people who will "represent our culture and appreciate the culture they are visiting."

And the organization hopes that scholars who return stay involved with the program, speaking to future applicants and even becoming Rotarians themselves.

Parents' union. Many unions also sponsor scholarships for the children of their members. Again, have your parents speak with the union officers about union-sponsored scholarships and other educational programs.

Church or religious organizations. Religious organizations may provide scholarships for members.

Local government. Often, local city council members and state representatives have a scholarship fund for the students of their district. Even if you didn't vote for them, call their offices and ask if they offer a scholarship.

Local businesses. Local businesses may provide awards to community members. Start inquiring at your local chamber of commerce or similar business organization.

Local newspaper. Most community newspapers make announcements about local students who win scholarships. Keep a record of the scholarship announcements or go to your library and look at back issues of the newspaper. Check last year's spring issues and you'll probably find announcements of scholarship recipients. Contact the sponsoring organizations to see if you're eligible to enter the next competition.

Which Scholarship Is Right For You?

Recently, a student wrote to us with a problem. He had conducted a search for scholarships on the Internet. He had anticipated finding a handful of awards to apply for but was shocked to find not handfuls but bucketfuls—over 100 potential scholarships. Unless he made applying for awards his full-time avocation, there was no way that he could apply for all of them.

You are likely to find yourself in a similar situation. Since there are tens of thousands of scholarships available, your problem may not be finding awards but deciding which ones to apply for and which you have the best chance of winning. Although there is no way to predict if you will win a scholarship, there are some methods you can use to select those that fit you best and therefore offer you the best chance of winning. Naturally, these are the ones for which you should apply.

The key is to realize that almost every scholarship organization has a mission or goal for giving away its money. Few groups give away free money for no reason. For example, a nature group might sponsor a scholarship with the goal of promoting conservation and encouraging students to be environmentally conscious. To this end the group will reward students who have demonstrated a concern for the environment and have some plan to contribute to this cause in the future.

Work Experience & Financial Aid
Knight Ridder Minority Scholars Program

Students who become Knight Ridder Minority Scholars not only receive a $40,000 scholarship, they also receive four summer internships and a full-time job after they graduate from college.

Nominated by one of the 31 local newspapers owned by Knight Ridder, scholars are selected in their senior year of high school. Even before they start college, the students work at a 12-week internship during the summer between their senior year of high school and freshman year of college. For the next three summers, the students intern for Knight Ridder and then work for the company for one year after they graduate.

"It's building a relationship between students and the company early on at a time when students want to learn more about the newspaper business," says Jacqui Love Marshall, vice president of human resources, diversity and development.

In addition to the internships and job opportunity, the students also meet annually at a Scholars Retreat. The retreat allows the students to meet executives of the company, interact with each other and gain additional training. A recent retreat brought the students to the conference of the Asian American Journalists Association and offered the students additional workshops on subjects such as workplace political skills, business social skills and strategic planning in the newspaper industry.

"For us it's a great opportunity to find new talent. For students it's a wonderful opportunity for them to get a diverse experience before graduating," Marshall says.

Understanding the mission of the scholarship is important because it will clue you into the kind of student the organization is looking for. If you have the background, interests and accomplishments that match this mission, then it is a scholarship you have a good chance of winning.

In our example of the nature group, if you are passionate about conservation, are active in the Sierra Club and know that you could write a compelling essay about your interest in global warming, then you would be a great candidate. If, on the other hand, you can't remember the last time you spent more than an hour outdoors, this award is not for you and you would be wasting your time by applying.

By knowing and understanding what the mission of the scholarship is, you can determine if you are the kind of student the committee wants to reward.

Their Mission Is Your Mission

There is no mystery to figuring out why organizations give away money. In most cases, the organizations come right out and tell you what they are trying to achieve with the award.

To find out, start by carefully reading the award description. Oftentimes organizations spell out what they are looking for in the description of who is eligible for the award. Sometimes they provide the criteria that they use for judging the competition. Criteria can include qualities such as academic achievement, community involvement, leadership and character.

The requirements for applying can also provide clues. Is there a minimum GPA? If there is and it's high, then academic achievement is probably important. Does the application provide a half page to list your activities? If so then they are probably a fairly significant part of the selection criteria. Do you need to submit an essay on a specific topic or a project to demonstrate your proficiency in a field of study? All of these requirements are clues about what the scholarship committee thinks is important.

After you read the application, research the awarding organization. What is the group's mission? Who are its members? What do they hope to accomplish? You can probably guess what kind of student will impress a group of physicists versus poets.

All things being equal, most clubs and organizations want to reward students who are most similar to their membership. If you

When & Where To Find Scholarships
Wiredscholar.com

The best advice that Michael Darne, director of business development for Wiredscholar, has for students is to start early and use both high and low tech search tools.

"It really helps to start early. Students should begin thinking about scholarships in their sophomore year," recommends Darne. Even if you are not able to apply for every award that you find, keeping a running list now will give you a huge advantage once you become a senior.

As for where to find scholarships, Darne recommends two distinctly different methods. "You can use a scholarship search engine like the Wiredscholar search engine," says Darne. But besides the Internet, Darne also advises to not overlook the people around you.

"Meet with your guidance counselor. They're going to know about most of the good local scholarships. Get the word out to everyone you know that you're going to college and you need the money. Some of these scholarships may not be big money, but $500 here or $1,000 there can add up quickly," he says.

don't know much about the organization, contact them to find out more. Check out their website. Read their brochures or publications. The more you know about why the organization is giving the award, the better you'll be able to understand how you may or may not fit.

Inside Information From Past Winners

One of the reasons why we study history is to apply the lessons learned from the past to the present. The same is true for gaining insight into scholarship competitions. One of the best ways to see who wins is to meet previous winner. Most organizations publicize the winners' names. However, it may be a little more difficult to get winners' phone numbers or e-mail addresses. We suggest providing your contact information to the organization to pass on to a winner and let him or her contact you first.

When you do make contact, learn as much as you can about the selection process and ask for advice. Don't forget to ask winners why they think they won. Often, their familiarity with the contest and experience of having gone through the competition will give them an impression of why they were selected.

Finding awards that match your background, achievements and interests is extremely important. All of the essay and interview strategies presented in the following chapters are most effective if you have spent time selecting awards that fit you best.

CHAPTER THREE

JUDGES' ROUNDTABLE:
INSIDE THE SELECTION PROCESS

In this chapter:

■ Get the scoop from real scholarship judges and experts

■ Discover how the selection process actually works

■ See who judges the competitions

■ Understand what makes the difference between being a winner and a runner-up

Meet Your Scholarship Judges

This is the first of three Judges' Roundtables in this book. We present these candid conversations with actual scholarship judges and experts so that you can hear in their own words what works and what doesn't.

Imagine that you were trying to win $1,000. One way to do this would be to buy a lottery ticket. Another way of doing this would be to apply for a scholarship. The difference between the two is that you cannot affect your chances of winning the lottery, but you can affect your chances of winning a scholarship.

When applying for scholarship competitions, one of the most important things to understand is why the organization is giving the award. Every organization has a reason for providing funds to students. These reasons can be quite varied. The organization may want to contribute to the communities in which it does business, increase the status of members of a minority or underrepresented group or build morale among its employees.

By understanding what the organization hopes to achieve through its scholarship program, you can develop essays and interview answers that best show how you fulfill the mission of the award. Here are some examples of purposes of scholarship programs. Try to imagine that you are applying to these awards and think about how knowing the purpose of each scholarship would help you to create a better application.

 What is the purpose of your award? Why are you giving away free money?

Georgina Salguero
Hispanic Heritage Awards Foundation
"Our mission is to promote and reward Hispanic excellence and to provide a greater understanding of the contribution of Hispanic Americans in the U.S. One way we do this is through identifying and rewarding outstanding youth who in turn will serve as the role models for other youth.

"In addition to a scholarship award, we also provide each winner with a $1,000 check to donate to an established nonprofit organization of the student's choice. This is a way for the student to give right back to the community, to never forget who they are and where they came from. After all, how many 17-year-olds do you know who have a way to thank the community that has helped them get to where they are?"

Cathy Edwards
Discover Financial Services Inc.
"We wanted to structure a program that would not only demonstrate our commitment to education but also invest in our children's futures."

Ellen Frishberg
Johns Hopkins University
"The Hodson award goes to students who present the best credentials in our incoming class academically and in leadership. We're looking not just for local leadership but leadership on a regional or national level."

Brent Drage
Rotary International Ambassadorial Scholarship Program
"Our scholarship program was started to further international understanding by providing money for students to study abroad. That's why we call our winners ambassadors. Recipients are expected to be ambassadors of good will."

Tracey Wong Briggs
All-USA Academic Teams
"Our program is really an editorial project for *USA Today*. What we are trying to do is tell the stories about what outstanding students can do. We are looking to reward students who have a good story to tell about something they have accomplished either academically and extracurricularly."

Marie M. Ishida
California Interscholastic Federation Scholar-Athlete of the Year
"We want to acknowledge and recognize outstanding scholars who are also good athletes."

Patricia R. Kovacs
Imation Computer Arts Scholarship Program
"Our award supports the use of technology in arts education and encourages creativity and innovation among the nation's high school students."

Jacqui Love Marshall
Knight Ridder Minority Scholars Program
"We're looking to find people early in their career planning who have an interest in newspapering, either journalism or working on the business side. We also want to raise interest and awareness about careers in newspapers among students."

Corisa Moreno
The Music Center Spotlight Awards
"Our award is meant to encourage high school students in the visual and performing arts to continue to follow their passion by providing support."

Wanda Carroll
National Association of Secondary School Principals
"We administer several awards that have different goals. For example, the Prudential Spirit of Community Award seeks to identify and honor middle level high school students on the basis of their volunteer work. For Wendy's High School Heisman Award we are looking to honor and promote both citizenship and athletic ability. For the Principal's Leadership Award we want to recognize an outstanding student leader."

Bob Murray
USA Funds
"Our scholarship program is aimed toward lower-income students in an attempt to narrow the gap in college attendance rates between lower-income and higher-income families."

 # Who typically judges the scholarship competition?

When applying for scholarships, it's important to keep in mind who the judges are. If you know that the judges will be local leaders, you may choose to focus on how you have contributed to your community. If you can, ask who will be on the selection committee. This may help you select which essay subject and interview topics of conversation are the most appropriate.

Georgina Salguero
Hispanic Heritage Awards Foundation
"Within the 12 cities of our regional competition we try to get local leaders to be the judges. For example, we work with the head of the chamber of commerce, people at various universities, clergy, civic leaders and other leaders within the community. We feel that these people know best how to evaluate the students in their communities."

Tracey Wong Briggs
All-USA Academic Teams
"For the high school competition, the judges include representatives from the National Education Association and National Association of Secondary School Principals. For the college competition, the judges include representatives from the American Council on Education, National Association of Independent Colleges and Universities, American Association of Colleges for Teacher Education and a former winner."

Laura DiFiore
FreSch! Free Scholarship Search
"I try to get a diverse group of people. Recent judges have included an Episcopalian minister, nurse, former librarian, substitute teacher, accountant, retired homemaker, computer programmer and high school junior."

Jacqui Love Marshall
Knight Ridder Minority Scholars Program
"We form our judging committee with two or three people at the corporate office level, sometimes a person from our local newspaper (*The San Jose Mercury News* or a Monterey newspaper) and then I usually ask someone from the community or local industry. Each year I aim to create a diverse committee."

Russ Hobbs
Rotary International Ambassadorial Scholarship Program
"We have a six-member judging panel. Three are former Ambas-

sadorial Scholars. The other three are Rotarians who have a love of the scholarship program."

Q How does your scholarship selection process work?

Understanding how the selection process works as well as realizing that not all competitions are the same will help you see where to focus your energies. If you can, learn about the scholarship program's selection process, what happens at each stage and how the applicants are evaluated.

Kimberly Hall
United Negro College Fund
"Students submit their applications directly to the UNCF. We perform a preliminary screening and send the strongest applications that we feel match the goals of specific donors on to those donors. Typically, the donor will then select the winner."

Trisha Bazemore
Coca-Cola Scholars Foundation
"The foundation first selects semifinalists based on a quantitative analysis of students' initial applications. Then, a 27-member Program Review Committee reviews the semifinalists' applications and essays. From this judging, 250 students are advanced as finalists. These students are then asked to travel to Atlanta at the expense of the Scholars Foundation to attend the Scholars Weekend, where they meet the other finalists and are interviewed by members of the National Selection Committee. Based on their applications and this interview, finalists are designated either as one of 50 National Scholars, receiving a four-year, $20,000 scholarship or as one of 200 Regional Scholars, receiving a four-year, $4,000 scholarship."

Corisa Moreno
The Music Center Spotlight Awards
"We start with our preliminary audition and there we screen for the basics. For example, let's say you're a singer. We would look for basic skills like tone and pitch. For dance we would look at the quality of your dance skills and musicality. As the applicants

advance, the competition gets more intense because you've got a handful of very qualified dancers and musicians. At the final level everyone is extremely talented and what often makes the winner stand out is that extra level of professional persona."

Janet L. Horowitz
Tyco Capital is Pro Education Program
"Each of the 10 eligible high schools in the Newark, New Jersey, area submits a candidate. The students meet with employees of Tyco who interview them one on one. The students also have 15 minutes to write an essay before their interview. Based on this interview and the short essay we select the winners."

Patricia R. Kovacs
Imation Computer Arts Scholarship Program
"The initial screening is performed as a class project by students from the Minneapolis College of Art and Design. A team of 7 students reviews over 500 applications, narrowing them down to 100 based on criteria that include creativity, uniqueness, color and quality. A panel of eight professional judges is then called upon to select the winners."

Tracey Wong Briggs
All-USA Academic Teams
"We have two steps. The preliminary judges score each applicant against a score sheet. That's why it's real important for people to read the nomination form carefully since every item on the nomination form is what we are judging for on the score sheet. During the finals, the judges meet and they try to build an academic team. They read all of the finalist applications and pick the first, second and third teams."

Wanda Carroll
National Association of Secondary School Principals
"When you are dealing with thousands of applications, you have to find a way to narrow the field. All of the applications are screened using an algorithm. We determine a set number of criteria that they have to meet and a certain number of points that they need to have to be considered for the finals. We narrow down our applicants to the top 1,000 or 2,000 applications. Each application is then read by a team of readers. A team will select a state and read all of the applications from that state. The num-

ber of awards for a specific state is based on the population of that state."

Laura DiFiore
FreSch! Free Scholarship Search
"There are two stages for the judging. I personally pull out the no go's. These are the applicants that on first glance are clearly not qualified to move forward in the competition. Those that pass this stage are sent to judging. During the judging stage you have to impress all 10 judges. We use a point scale, and the winning applicant and essay has received the highest marks from all of the judges. We usually pick out the winner in about three hours. The second and third prize tend to take us two days. Out of all the entries, there will be about 50 stories and 70 poems going to final judging."

Q What qualities do you look for when selecting the winner?

If you know what qualities the organization is seeking in the winner, you can highlight those achievements that best showcase these qualities. Carefully read the organization's literature, website and publications to figure out what the judges seek. Or contact the organization directly to ask. Imagine how much stronger your application will be if you apply for these awards and know what the judges themselves think is most important.

Bob Murray
USA Funds
"In addition to the income requirement, we consider past academic performance and future potential, leadership, participation in school and community activities, work experience and career and educational aspirations and goals. Each of these additional criteria carry approximately equal weight."

Janet L. Horowitz
Tyco Capital is Pro Education Program
"The company seeks to give to students who may not be able to attend college without outside scholarships. We also look for students who give of their time to the community. In fact, we re-

quire that every student who wins our award must give back at least 20 hours of community service. We want to give our money to students who want to make a difference in the community."

Trisha Bazemore
Coca-Cola Scholars Foundation
"We are primarily looking at overall achievements in leadership, not only in school activities but also within their communities."

Georgina Salguero
Hispanic Heritage Awards Foundation
"Because the students select from seven career or talent categories in which to enter, the selection committee asks, 'Do we see this student excelling in this category 10 years from now?' With any selection, the cream rises to the top. We look at their academics, community service, leadership, as well as their fit and potential within their category."

Jacqui Love Marshall
Knight Ridder Minority Scholars Program
"We're looking for primarily academic strength. This is a person who is likely to do well in college so they won't be struggling. We also want a person who has a genuine interest in either journalism or the newspaper business."

Cathy Edwards
Discover Financial Services Inc.
"We're asking students to not only list community service efforts but to describe why they've been meaningful. It makes them stop and reflect. It helps them demonstrate their well-roundedness. It's not the students who have the highest GPA. We're trying to help the students who might not have scholarship dollars available to them."

Tracey Wong Briggs
All-USA Academic Teams
"The judges are looking for how you use your intellectual skills outside of the classroom, how you take academic excellence beyond getting an 'A' in class. Judges ask things like how are you using the knowledge that you're gaining in the classroom? Do you have a rigorous curriculum and are you challenging yourself?"

Corisa Moreno
The Music Center Spotlight Awards
"We look at the end result. Our past finalists are at a very professional level. A lot of them go on to major dance companies and institutions such as Julliard. They are at that professional level where you could stick them on a stage anywhere and they would be a crowd pleaser."

Laura DiFiore
FreSch! Free Scholarship Search
"We're looking for originality and creativity, what we call the goosebump effect. When you get to the last sentence of the essay, you lean back and say 'wow.'"

Wanda Carroll
National Association of Secondary School Principals
"The National Honor Society Scholarships are based on the students' character, service and leadership as exemplified in their application and essay. As the name suggests, winners for the Principal's Leadership Award are selected based on their leadership. Our selection committee seeks a student who is class president, who is involved in athletics being captain or co-captain or who demonstrates community service as the head of their youth group. In short we are looking for someone who is obviously showing leadership qualities. The Prudential Spirit of Community Award, on the other hand, is based entirely on community service. One recent winner started a *Suitcases for Kids* program to provide suitcases for children in homeless shelters to move their belongings."

Russ Hobbs
Rotary International Ambassadorial Scholarship Program
"We're not looking for that person who has a 4.0 GPA and spends all his time in the library. We're looking for the people who want to give something back to the community, people who we hope will make a difference in the world and who believe in the values that we believe in Rotary. It's our hope that at some point in the future our winners will become Rotarians."

Q What sets the winner apart from the runner-up?

One of the most frequent observations from scholarship judges is that there are many more students qualified to win than there are scholarships available. This means that they must look for that little something extra to separate the winners from the almost winners. Here is some guidance to help you understand what can set you apart from the other applicants.

Shirley Kennedy Keller
American Association of School Administrators
"It's about what the students have accomplished in more than just one area of their lives. We believe that success in life is more than a GPA. It's also what you can accomplish in your personal life, in your community. We're looking for the best all-around applicants. We're looking for students who are going to be successful in their lives."

Janet L. Horowitz
Tyco Capital is Pro Education Program
"Their attitude is number one. A positive attitude, a student who you know is going to make it no matter what. This is what separates the winners from the runner-ups."

Corisa Moreno
The Music Center Spotlight Awards
"They really have to enjoy what they're doing. That comes off quite a bit in their performances. You can see when they have a deep love for their art form."

Patricia R. Kovacs
Imation Computer Arts Scholarship Program
"We're getting such high-quality projects that it's very difficult for us to select the winner. Being creative and using color creatively are probably what ultimately helps us to decide which project deserves to win."

Brent Drage
Rotary International Ambassadorial Scholarship Program
"Students who have a little more concrete plan tend to edge out

others who don't. We understand that at that age you need to be flexible about your future, but we also want to see that you have some grasp on where you're headed."

Q What advice do you have for future applicants?

Some of the best advice you can get is from those who will be judging your scholarship applications. Since many have seen hundreds if not thousands of applications, they see firsthand how you can find awards, create a powerful application and essay and avoid the mistakes that other students make.

Kimberly Hall
United Negro College Fund
"Start looking for scholarships and applying early. I encourage students to start in their sophomore year of high school. Of course, they can start even earlier than that too."

Tracey Wong Briggs
All-USA Academic Teams
"Pursue the interests you love. One of the things we see that always comes out are students who just care so much about what they're doing. If you do that, the awards will come."

Mario A. De Anda
Hispanic Scholarship Fund
"Read the application before you start filling it out. Spend time on the personal statement. It's our first impression of you so it needs to be good."

Wanda Carroll
National Association of Secondary School Principals
"There is nothing that disqualifies a student quicker than not following instructions. Make sure that all the signatures are there. Make sure you have every 'i' dotted and every 't' crossed. We have hundreds each year who don't make the first cutoff. It's not that they are not qualified but they just haven't followed the instructions."

Russ Hobbs
Rotary International Ambassadorial Scholarship Program
"Sell us on the things that you have done outside of the academic area. You need to let us know why we should want to fund you over 30 or 40 other candidates in our district."

Ellen Frishberg
Johns Hopkins University
"Focus and do well. We're looking for the academic program not just grades. We also want to see that students do well in activities and that they don't just join lots of organizations for the sake of listing them on their application. Focus on leadership since this award tends to go to students who invented, chaired, captained or did something that shows leadership."

Laura DiFiore
FreSch! Free Scholarship Search
"The bottom line is that we want to give you the money. It's up to you to give us a reason to say 'yes.' Please, please, please give us reasons to say 'yes.'"

Participating Judges & Experts

Trisha Bazemore, Program Assistant, Coca-Cola Scholars Foundation

Tracey Wong Briggs, Coordinator, *USA Today* All-USA Academic and Teacher Teams

Wanda Carroll, Program Manager, National Association of Secondary School Principals

Mario A. De Anda, Director of Scholarship Programs, Hispanic Scholarship Fund

Laura DiFiore, Founder, FreSch! Free Scholarship Search Let's Get Creative Short Story and Poetry Scholarship Contest

Brent Drage, Resource Development Assistant, Rotary International Ambassadorial Scholarship Program

Cathy Edwards, Manager, Public Relations and Charitable Sponsorships, Discover Financial Services Inc.

Ellen Frishberg, Director of Student Financial Services, Johns Hopkins University

Kimberly Hall, Peer Program Manager, United Negro College Fund

Russ Hobbs, District Scholarship Chairman, Rotary International Ambassadorial Scholarship Program

Janet L. Horowitz, Assistant Vice President of Corporate Philanthropy, Tyco Capital is Pro Education Program

Marie M. Ishida, Executive Director, California Interscholastic Federation (CIF) Scholar-Athlete of the Year

Shirley Kennedy Keller, Program Director, American Association of School Administrators, which administers the Discover Card Tribute Award Scholarship

Patricia R. Kovacs, Community Affairs Manager, Imation Computer Arts Scholarship Program

Jacqui Love Marshall, Vice President of Human Resources, Diversity and Development, Knight Ridder Minority Scholars Program

Corisa Moreno, Project Coordinator, The Music Center Spotlight Awards

Bob Murray, Manager of Corporate Communications, USA Funds

Georgina Salguero, Senior Manager, Programs and Events, Hispanic Heritage Youth Awards

HOW TO WRITE A MONEY-WINNING ESSAY

In this chapter:

■ Why the essay is critical

■ What judges look for in your scholarship essay

■ The three common features of all money-winning essays

■ How to find the perfect topic

■ The keys to crafting a powerful essay

■ Why sob stories don't work

■ Hard to believe but true essay mistakes

■ How to recycle your essay

Why The Essay Is Critical To Winning

Let's imagine for a moment that you are a scholarship judge. You have an enormous pile of applications in front of you. From the application forms, you can get basic information about each of the students such as grades, test scores and brief descriptions of their activities.

But without being able to meet each candidate, how do you get a sense of who they are and determine if they are the most deserving of your money? One of the best (and sometimes only) ways to get to know the applicants beyond their cut and dry statistics is through their essays.

This is why for many scholarship competitions the essay is the most important part of your application and where you should spend the most time. Scholarship judges view the essay as their window into who you are, your passions and your potential. It is their way of getting to know you without actually meeting you. And it is where you can make the strongest and most meaningful impression.

There are some interesting implications depending on the type of student that you are. If you are a straight "A" student with excellent test scores and a flawless academic record, you may be tempted to rely on these achievements to carry your application all the way to the final round. However, if you neglect to spend the time and effort on your essay, your achievements may advance you beyond the preliminary round, but you won't win the big prize.

On the other hand, if you are an average student and know that other applicants will have better academic achievements than you, then you can use the opportunity that the essay provides to make yourself stand out. In many cases you will actually be able to beat applicants who have higher GPAs and test scores.

Regardless of your accomplishments and academic achievements, if you want to win a scholarship you need to write a powerful essay.

Focus On Solutions
United Negro College Fund

Some students seem to think that the more tears they can get the selection committee to shed, the better their chances will be to win. It's true that scholarship judges will feel sympathy for students who have gone through difficult times. But they will reward those who have done so and succeeded or who have a plan for succeeding despite these obstacles.

In the over 400 scholarship programs that the United Negro College Fund administers, essays play an important role. "It gives you a sense of who the student is and what they want to do with the money if they win. It gives you more of a picture of the student as a whole as opposed to just a name," says Kimberly Hall, peer program manager.

While many students write about serious issues or hardships, Hall advises students to take a positive approach when writing their essays. Instead of focusing only on their problems, students should explain what they have faced and then describe their plan of action for the future. The best essays have a sense of "purpose and direction," she says.

The Making Of A Powerful Essay

Every summer there is a blockbuster adrenaline-laden action movie complete with pumped-up action hero, oversized guns and unbelievable car chases. In the midst of exploding buildings and the hero tearing away in a red sports car, it would be out of place for the background music to be a polka. The sights and sounds of the movie need to fit together to create the desired atmosphere. If one element is out of place, like a polka during the climax of an action scene, it destroys the effect of the entire movie.

Similarly, what makes a good essay is that it is developed to fit within the context of the overall application. In other words, the essay and all other elements in your application package such as your list of activities and educator recommendations must fit together to create the effect you want.

Let's say that you are applying for an award based on community service. In your application you list all of the community service groups that you belong to and service project awards that you've won. But in your essay you vent about your disgust for the homeless and how they should find jobs instead of blocking your passage on sidewalks. Your essay may be brilliantly conceived and written, but if its message is not in line with the rest of your application it will create a conflicting presentation and keep you out of the winners' bracket.

Even if we reverse this example, the result is the same. Imagine that you wrote a brilliant essay about community service but had no related activities to back up the commitment you profess in your essay. The essay, no matter how well written, will not make up for a lack of actual involvement in community service work.

When you think about your essay, consider it within the context of your entire application. You want to present a cohesive message with the essay as the centerpiece. Each piece of your application should support your overall message.

At this point many students ask, "How do I know what the message or theme of my essay and application should be?" The answer is actually quite simple and goes back to why you decided to apply for the scholarship in the first place.

The theme of your essay and application is almost always determined by the goal of the award, why the organization is giving away the money.

For example, a minority advocacy organization may provide an award to help members of its underrepresented ethnic group to pursue a higher education. A private foundation may give an award to preserve the memory of a late benefactor who supported students entering teaching. A professional organization may award money to encourage students to enter their profession.

If you read Chapter 2 about finding scholarships you already know that it's important to research and uncover the purpose of each award. Now you can use this information to guide your essay and application.

Once you know the goal of the organization, use that knowledge to choose which aspect of your life to highlight and therefore the general theme of your essay. If you were applying for the award for underrepresented students, you'd want to focus on your potential and how you will be a role model for others in your group in the future. To apply for the educator or other professional award, you'd want to highlight your future in education or the field of the awarding organization. In other words, use the goal of the award as a guide for your essay.

Three Common Features Of All Money-Winning Essays

Let's imagine that you have done your research on the scholarship organization and have a sense of why they are giving away their money. You have even thought of a few themes that you might use when applying for the award. No matter what you write about, we have found that there are qualities that are shared by all successful scholarship essays. As you write, keep the following points in mind.

#1 Originality

For your essay to be a winner, it needs to be original. Remember that your essay will be among thousands of other essays that are being judged. If your essay does not stand out from the rest, it will be forgotten along with your chances of winning.

There are two ways that you can be original. The first is to find a unique topic. Think about what makes you, well, you. What point of view or life experience can you share that is unique? One expert we know uses the thumb test. Place your thumb over the name at the top of the essay, and ask yourself if the author could be one of many students. If so then the essay is probably not original.

Unfortunately, finding a unique topic is very difficult which leads us to the second way that you can be original. Instead of racking your brains to come up with a 100% original topic, take an ordinary topic but approach it in an original way. For example, if you were writing about how your mother is your role model you would not want to approach it in the same way that everyone else will. Don't write about how you love your mother and she loves you. Chances are many applicants will write similar things about their parents. Instead, spend some time thinking about what it is specifically that makes your mother a role model. Maybe it's because of her secret recipe for meatloaf or the way she hums while cleaning or how she falls asleep in front of the television with the remote control still in her hand. We all have experiences that make us and those who surround us unique, and the key is to zero in on these and use them in your scholarship essays.

One way to insure that your essay is original is to avoid common topics or approaches of other essay writers. In fact, these mistakes are so common that we have an entire chapter devoted to them. Be sure to carefully study the essays in Chapter 6, *12 Essays That Bombed,* to make sure that your topic or approach does not resemble any of these failures.

#2 Answer The Underlying Question

Have you ever been asked one question but felt like there was an underlying question that was really being asked? Maybe a parent has asked you something like, "Tell me about your new friend Karen." But what your parent is really asking is, "Tell me about your new friend Karen. Are her 12 earrings and tattoo-laden arms a sign that you shouldn't be spending so much time with her?"

In most cases the essay question is just a springboard for you to answer the real question the scholarship judges want answered. An organization giving an award for students who plan to study business might ask, "Why do you want to study business?" But the underlying question they are asking is, "Why do you want to study business, and why are you the best future business person we should give our hard earned money to?"

For every scholarship you will be competing with students who share similar backgrounds and goals. If you are applying to an

Hard To Believe But True Essay Mistakes
FreSch! Let's Get Creative Scholarship Contest

Laura DiFiore, the founder of FreSch! Free Scholarship Search, has seen many mistakes. Some of these mistakes have prompted her to separate essays into three piles, the good, the bad and the ugly. Those essays designated as the ugly are put into a box with a tombstone drawn on it.—Gen and Kelly

Bathroom humor. One applicant wrote an entire essay about excrement. "It met the requirements of originality but not creativity. It was gross."

Spelling mistakes. "While some mistakes are tolerated, if you can't spell your own major, you're not getting a scholarship."

Inferior, illegible printing. DiFiore received an essay in which the middle section of the applicant's printing ribbon ran out. This meant that she could only see the top third and bottom third of each letter. The entire middle of all of the letters was totally illegible.

Plagiarism. During a recent competition, DiFiore received essays from applicants who took last year's winning essay which was posted on her website, modified it and submitted it as their own.

Copycats. DiFiore received essays from three sisters who all wrote the same basic story.

Threats. One essay writer threatened the selection committee, "If you don't give me money I'm going to hunt you down."

Anonymous applicants. DiFiore has received applications with no name or address on them. It's difficult to award a scholarship to an anonymous applicant.

award that supports students who want to become doctors you can bet that 99% of the students applying also want to become doctors. Therefore, the goal of every scholarship judge is to determine who is the *best* applicant out of a pool of applicants who at first glance look very similar.

So let's distill the underlying question that the scholarship judges really want answered. That is: Why do you deserve to win? (Your answer should not be, "Because I need the money!")

Think about these two hypothetical questions: The Farmers Association asks you to write about the future of farming. The Historical Society asks you to describe the importance of history. While at first these two questions seem unrelated they are both driving at the same thing: Tell us why you deserve to win.

In answering either of these questions, you would need to address the underlying question. When writing the Farmers Association essay, you could discuss the general condition of farms and farmers but you'd better be sure to include how you fit into the future of farming. Similarly when answering the Historical Society's question you could write about history in any way you please but you should also include if not focus on your own past and future contributions to the field of historical research or preservation. Use the essay question as a way to prove to the scholarship committee that you are the worthiest applicant for the award.

#3 Passion

As a student you have written a lot of essays. And let's be honest. Most were probably on topics you didn't care much about. You might be tempted to approach the scholarship essay in the same way that you did when you wrote about the Roman Aqueducts. This would be a tragic mistake. The last common feature of all money-winning essays is that they are written on subjects about which the author is truly passionate.

It is very difficult to fake passion for a subject. But when you are genuinely enthusiastic about something it also does not take much effort for that energy to naturally show through in your writing. Therefore, when you are choosing what to write about be sure it is something you truly care about and are interested in. Without even trying, you will find that your sentences convey an excitement that the reader can feel.

When you read the examples of the actual essays in Chapter 5, *30 Money-Winning Essays*, you will quickly see that the writers all cared deeply for their topics.

How To Find The Perfect Topic

When we were taught to color inside the lines, our artwork may have been neater but it was at the expense of creativity. The best time-tested method to develop creative ideas on what to write about is through brainstorming. By thinking without restrictions, creativity flourishes. We have found that the best way to do this is to keep a notebook with you and write down ideas for topics whenever they pop into your head. Also set aside some time for a dedicated brainstorm session where you force yourself to generate new ideas.

The key to having a successful brainstorming session is to not be critical of the topics you write down. Let your imagination roam. Also, ask your parents and friends for suggestions.

The one shortcoming of brainstorming is that sometimes a good idea does not make for a good essay. It may be too complex to write about within the limitations of the essay requirements.

The only way to really tell if an idea is good is to start writing. So from your list of ideas pick several that you feel are the most promising and start composing an essay. Again, don't pay attention to the quality of the writing just yet. You are basically testing the topic to see if it has the potential to make a great essay.

If you get stuck and think the topic may not work then set it aside and try another. We have found that most students will try and then abandon two or three ideas for every good one they find. That means that you need a long list of ideas and must be willing to cut your losses and ditch a topic that does not pan out.

Essay Writing Tips

When it comes time to write, the best way to start is like removing a bandage. Just do it, and do it quickly. To help, here are some strategies for writing.

Remember To Focus On Originality
While it is not always possible to come up with an original topic–

especially if the question is the same for everyone—make sure that your essay contains originality.

If you are writing about involvement in a sport, don't use common topics like how sports taught you the value of teamwork or how you scored the winning touchdown, goal or point. These are common topics and if you use them you risk having your essay lost among the hundreds of others that sound similar. It's perfectly fine to write about common topics like sports, but think of a different angle. Maybe you had a unique experience or can focus on an aspect of athletics that is often overlooked.

Another common mistake is general statements. Be specific. Don't write, "education is the key to success." Instead, give the judges a slice of your life. Show them how education has impacted your life in a single experience or realization.

If you are writing about your desire to become an astronaut you might explain how this began when your father bought you a model rocket for Christmas. Focusing on a specific example of your life will help readers relate to your experiences and insure that your essay is memorable and original.

Share Something Personal
While some questions ask you to write about a national or international problem or event, the scholarship committee still would like to know something about you. After all, you are the one they are giving their money to.

Some of the better essays that we have seen written about serious issues like drug abuse or nuclear nonproliferation have also found ways to incorporate the author. One student who wrote about the U.S. arms policy spoke about his personal involvement in a club at school that hosts an annual peace conference. He was able to tie in the large international policy issues with the more personal aspect of what he was doing on an individual level. It was a great policy essay, which also revealed something about the author.

Test Your Thesis With A Simple Question
It sounds obvious, but many students' essays don't have a clear point. Whether you are describing the influence of your father or

The Importance Of Going Beyond The Superficial
Knight Ridder Minority Scholars Program

To apply for the Knight Ridder Minority Scholars Program, students must write a personal statement. Many turn to the Knight Ridder website to get background information on the company. For some, this is a mistake.

"You realize they went to the site and cut and pasted material from it into their essay. But it's clear that they have little idea what these facts mean," says Jacqui Love Marshall, vice president of human resources, diversity and development.

The students cite statistics about the number of newspapers owned by Knight Ridder or the number of Pulitzer Prizes the media company has won. She adds, "It's almost the difference between writing a book report by having read the Cliffsnotes versus having read the book."

What's more important than regurgitating statistics found on an awarding organization's website is finding a personal connection to the organization.

"When you're looking at dozens of these essays in the middle of the night you begin to differentiate between someone who put their heart and soul in it, that there is a level of commitment there versus essays that have all the requisite information but not a personal involvement," says Marshall.

the effect of World War II on race relations, you must have a central idea that you communicate to the reader.

To see if your essay has a central thesis, try this simple exercise. Ask yourself, "In a single sentence what is the point of my essay?" Here are some answers that would satisfy the question:

"Growing up in the country taught me to be independent."
"Treatment of addiction is the only way to win the war on drugs."

If you cannot answer this question with a single sentence then your main point may not be clear enough. Or worse, your essay may not have one.

Expand On Your Accomplishments

Winning a scholarship is about impressing the judges and showing them why you are the best candidate. Your accomplishments, activities, talents and awards all help to prove that you are the best fit. Since you will probably list your activities on the application form, you can use your essay to expand on one or two of the most important.

However, don't just parrot back what is on your application. Use the opportunity to focus on a specific accomplishment, provide detail and to put it into the proper context. Listing on your application that you were a stage manager for a play does not explain that you also had to design and build all of the sets in a week. The essay allows you to expand on an achievement to demonstrate its significance.

Beware Of Meaningless Facts

Some students approach the essay like a research paper, cramming it with statistics and survey results. You might think that the facts and figures wow judges. While this does display research skills, by itself it hardly makes for a good essay. In particular, if you are trying to impress a corporation with your knowledge of their sales and global markets, don't just repeat facts you found on their website. If you are going to use facts about the sponsoring organization be sure that they are essential to your essay. Don't repeat statistics without a reason, and don't think that the more you have the better.

Don't Write A Sob Story

Tear-jerking stories may be popular subjects for television specials and song lyrics, but they rarely, if ever, win scholarships. A common theme students write about is why they need the scholarship money to continue their education. While this is a perfectly legitimate topic, it is often answered with an essay filled with family tragedies and hardships, a sob story. Again, there is nothing wrong with writing about this topic but don't expect to win if the intent of your essay is to evoke pity.

If your main point (remember our test) is: "I deserve money because of the suffering I've been through," you have a problem. Scholarship committees are not as interested in your problems as they are in your solutions. What have you accomplished despite these hardships? How have you succeeded despite the challenges you've faced? This is more significant and memorable than merely cataloging your misfortunes.

Plus, don't forget that to win you have to be an original. The sob story is one of the more common types of essays and it is hard to compete when you are telling the same story that literally hundreds of other students are also writing. Remember that every

An Essay Pop Quiz
Tyco Capital Is Pro Education Program

If you've had trouble writing an essay over the course of several days or weeks, consider that the 10 finalists in the Tyco Capital is Pro Education scholarship competition have only 15 minutes. Sure the students are told in advance that they will need to write an essay, but there's still a lot of pressure to perform when a $10,000 scholarship and internship opportunity hang in the balance.

"This format almost guarantees that we are getting their thoughts right off the top of their heads. We want to know what is truly important to them," says Janet L. Horowitz, assistant vice president of corporate philanthropy.

Recently the students were asked to either write about a day in their life 30 years later or what one thing they would change in the world if they had the ability. Even though their time is limited, the students have produced thoughtful pieces.

Horowitz points to one memorable essay in which the student described how she was the first female president 30 years from now.

"We're pretty open with how they do it. There are no mistakes," she adds.

applicant has faced difficulties. What's different and individual to you is how you've overcome those difficulties.

Show Some Positive Energy

Mom has probably said: If you don't have anything nice to say, don't say anything at all. Everyone likes an uplifting story. Especially, since you have your entire future ahead of you, scholarship judges want to feel your enthusiasm.

Try to stay away from essays that are overly pessimistic, antagonistic or critical. This doesn't mean that you have to put a happy spin on every word that you write or that you can't write about a serious problem. But it does mean that you should not concentrate only on the negative. If you are writing about a problem try to present some solutions.

Your optimism is what makes organizations excited about giving you money to pursue your passion for changing the world. Don't shy away from this fact.

The Importance Of Editors

There is an old writer's saying: Behind every good writer is an even better editor. If you want to create a masterpiece, you need the help of others. You don't need a professional editor or even someone who is a Shakespearean-level writer. You just need people who can read your work and give you useful constructive feedback.

Roommates, friends, family members, teachers, professors or advisors make great editors. When you get others to read your essay, they will find errors that you missed and help you make your essay clearer to someone who is not familiar with your topic.

You will find that some editors catch grammar and spelling mistakes but will not comment on the overall quality of the essay. Others will miss the technical mistakes but give you great advice on making the substance of your essay better. You need to find both types of editors.

Use Examples & Illustrate
Mark R. Eadie, Coca-Cola Scholars Regional Winner

"Make sure to use examples to illustrate points. Instead of saying 'I was active in high school,' describe your high school activities. Also, focus on one or two activities that had special meaning to you.

"There's a fine line between bragging and too much humility. Be honest about yourself and what you've done, and the scholarship committee will recognize this. Your essay is going to be read by real people who are intelligent and wise so don't make things up. Trying to trick them is like trying to trick parents; it just doesn't work.

"Also, the essay readers may have to read hundreds of essays, so give them something to remember you by."

As you find others to help improve your essay, be careful that they do not alter your work so much that your voice is lost. Editing is essential but your writing should always be your own.

Recycle & Reuse

This has no relation to aluminum cans or newspapers. What we mean is that you should reuse essays that you have written for college applications, classes or even other scholarships. Writing a good essay takes a lot of time and effort. As much as possible when you have a good essay you'll want to edit it and reuse it.

To recycle an essay try experimenting with changing the introduction. You may find that while you might have to write a few new paragraphs you can still use the body of your original essay.

One word of caution: don't try to recycle an essay when it just doesn't fit. The essay must answer the question. It's better to spend the extra time to write an appropriate essay than to submit one that doesn't match the scholarship.

How To Write A Great Introduction & Conclusion

Great novels have two things in common—a gripping introduction and a conclusion that leaves you something to think about when you're finished. Great essays share similar traits.

The first impression that the judges get is from your introduction. If it does not catch their attention and make them want to read further then you will lose even before you had a chance. Here are some strategies for starting:

Create action or movement. Use an example or short story to create action right at the beginning. Have you noticed how most movies begin with a striking scene that quickly draws you in? You need to do the same with your introduction.

Pose a question. Questions draw attention as the readers think about their answers and are curious to see how you answer them in your essay. You can also use an interesting or surprising fact in place of a question.

Describe. If you can create a vivid image for readers, they will be more likely to want to read on. Just be sure to do so succinctly since you don't want your introduction to be filled with detail that does not move the plot forward.

Conclusions are just as important as introductions since they are the last impression you will leave with your reader. Here are a few tips for your closing remarks.

Be thoughtful. Your conclusion should end with something insightful. You may even decide to withhold a thought from your essay so that you have something for your conclusion.

Don't just summarize. Since the reader has just finished your essay, there is no need for a summary. It's okay to summarize in one sentence, but try to add to it by making an extra point or consideration.

Essays Get Better With Each Revision
Kristin N. Javaras, Rhodes Scholar

"I highly recommend showing your essay to people who have won fellowships themselves or who have read successful fellowship application essays before (and the more people the better). I feel that the revision process was crucial for my essay: I went through about seven or eight drafts of my personal statement before I was satisfied!"

Don't be too quick to end. Too many students tack on a meaningless conclusion or even worse, don't have one at all. Have a decent conclusion that connects with the rest of your essay and that doesn't consist of two words, "The End."

As you look at your essay ask yourself: Will they think about what you have said after they have finished reading? If the answer is yes, then you have written a conclusion that you can be proud of.

CHAPTER FIVE

30 MONEY-WINNING ESSAYS

In this chapter:

■ **30 real essays about challenges, family, issues, community service, career plans, leadership, academics, athletics and artistic talents**

■ **Learn from and be inspired by these successful essays**

The Money-Winning Essays

You sit down at the computer, eyes focused on the monitor and fingers poised above the keyboard. You are ready to start writing your money-winning scholarship essay. But something is missing. Aha! What you need is inspiration.

In this chapter, we want to give you this inspiration. One of the best ways to learn how to write a successful essay is to read actual essays that won. While there is no single way to write a winning essay, you will find that most successful essays share traits such as originality, demonstrating why the author deserves to win and passion.

As you read these essays imagine that you are a scholarship judge. What image of the writer does the essay create? How do the essays make you feel? Would you give away your money to these writers?

Remember, unlike a creative writing assignment, the goal of a scholarship essay is to show the scholarship committee why you deserve to win. Keep in mind that these essays are meant to be examples of what worked for these particular students. Naturally, your essays will be individual to you. While your essays will surely differ in style, tone, language and subject matter, they should convey the same powerful impressions.

Ultimately, we want you to use these successful essays as inspiration to help you to write your own masterpiece.

Experiences & Challenges

Brian C. Babcock, Marshall & Truman Scholarship Winner

The path to becoming a Marshall Scholar and Truman Scholar is a long one. Brian's journey began at Bowie High School in Bowie, Maryland, when he was elected the president of the Russian Club. Since that time, he has studied at the U.S. Military Academy at West Point and worked as a Russian linguist.

Brian is one of 40 students in the nation to win the Marshall Scholarship and one of 80 students to win the Truman Scholarship. With the Marshall Scholarship, he will study at Oxford after graduating. Brian plans to use the $30,000 Truman Award to support his future graduate studies in foreign service and history and would eventually like to become the Defense Attache to Russia, working with the governments of the former Soviet republics to assist them in dismantling their nuclear, biological and chemical weapons. In this essay for the Truman Scholarship, he describes how at age 17 he embarked on a hike of the Appalachian Trail from Maine to Georgia. The solo hike lasted six months.

Lessons From The Outdoors

The outdoors has always played a large role in my life, whether in Boy Scouts, on my own or with the military thus far. However, there is one outdoor experience of mine that did not involve my being in a club. I also did not get any awards for this experience, yet it has had a more profound impact on who I am than any other single event in my life, my "thru-hike" of the Appalachian Trail from Maine to Georgia.

I started my thru-hike when I was 17 years old, three weeks after I graduated from high school. It took me just over six months to complete. In those six months, I learned more about myself than in the previous 17 years or in the five years since. There is nothing with which it can compare.

Brian's contributions reflect his own opinions, not those of the U.S. military.

I financed the hike with money that I saved during my last semester of high school, working 40 hours per week on top of my full-time student schedule. I was determined to reach Maine and hike south to Georgia. This was the first real goal that I had ever made for myself, and I reached it alone on a cold January morning.

The lessons from the trail are ones that have affected me in everything I have done since. Because of those six months, I see the world differently, in a way that is sometimes impossible to explain to someone else, though I might try.

My life was not difficult growing up, but I found a need to put myself through the difficulties of trail life. From this time, I gained an appreciation for the little things, like clean water to drink and a dry place to sleep (both of which were sometimes lacking). I met people from all walks of life, as they crossed paths with my walk in life. From that experience I am better able to deal with those whose backgrounds do not resemble mine, a skill I have used often in the military.

Now I have turned my life 180 degrees. I no longer have hair to the middle of my back or a beard. I have traded my Birkenstock sandals for combat boots. Yet, somehow, everything I did on the trail applies to what I have done since. Whether it's suffering in a foxhole during field training, or sleeping in a cold, dank lean-to on my hike, the lessons are not all that different.

Though my journey in life has wandered back onto the beaten path, I know that if the nation needs me to lead soldiers into the brush or assist in providing humanitarian aid, I have my previous experience to draw from. Because I have been there, I have a common bond of suffering with millions throughout the world and another bond to all of my soldiers. I am still amazed at how my former life as a free-spirited wanderer has better prepared me for life as a disciplined soldier.

Daniel Heras, Scantron Scholarship Winner

Daniel dreams of becoming a teacher to inspire students to learn in the same way that he has been inspired by his teachers. In this essay, he describes one of the most meaningful experiences he has had in high school through the Environmental Science Club, which took him to real life locales to learn about science not from textbooks but from seeing, touching and experiencing science first hand. Student body president and captain of the baseball team at Woodrow Wilson High School in Los Angeles, Daniel won over $17,000 in scholarships to attend U.C. Berkeley.

Inspired To Teach

In the ninth grade, I was introduced to the Environmental Science Club and to Mr. Quezada, my science teacher and advisor. Outside of the classroom and through the club, I saw an entirely different side to education. The science club took me to far and exotic destinations, such as the Islands of Hawaii, the underwater wonderlands of the Cayman Islands, the temperate climates of the Florida Everglades, the deep blue waters of the Mexican Riviera and the High Sierras of Northern California.

We learned that one cannot experience these things in class behind a small cramped desk made for 10-year-olds. I was able to hold, smell and sometimes taste, foreign artifacts. I have seen the migration patterns of the Humpback whale, have become a certified scuba diver, learned to surf, rock climb, snowboard and trail the mountains of the world, all while learning about science. Our trips have also given me the life skills of communication, learning to intermingle with people of the world.

It only took a year to see that teaching was my future. Why would someone not want to get paid for helping his or her community, to enlighten the future generation and best of all, do the things that bring joy to one's life all while on the job? I was given experiences I would not have received anywhere else, and I want to do the same for the next generation to come. There is a world that one can hold, smell and sometimes taste. I want to show people that there really is a world out there beyond the pictures in textbooks.

Mark R. Eadie, Coca-Cola Scholars Regional Winner

When Mark visits his 90-year-old grandmother, the two turn the volume on the television up. Though they are separated by almost 70 years in age, they share a similar problem: hearing impairment, Mark's grandmother because of age and Mark because of a childhood injury that left him partially deaf. This injury has not stopped Mark. If anything, it has sparked a passion to be a role model for others.

While a student at Columbia High School, Mark trained for hours as the lead of the school musical, perfecting his singing without the benefit of stereo hearing. The performance garnered rave reviews. From Rensselaer, New York, Mark received over $50,000 in scholarships to attend the University of Michigan, where he is a member of the national champion solar car team and is studying aerospace and mechanical engineering. He hopes that through his research in engineering he can develop solutions for others like him.

Invisible Handicap

Who would think a game of catch would change my life? At age 10 I lost hearing in one ear and had to struggle with the challenges resulting from this "invisible handicap." Through this I have become more sensitive to people's problems and handicaps, learned the value of my support community, refined career goals and challenged myself in new and difficult situations to help others.

My catching skills were not what my older brother thought, and his fast ball missed my glove and hit my cheek bone. After a severe concussion and cochlear surgery, I was totally deaf in the right ear. I had lost all stereophonic hearing and musicality. My voice started to become monotone. I could not tell from where sounds were coming, hear notes I was singing or

A Scholarship Support Network

Emanuel Pleitez, Recipient of $30,000 in Scholarships

Emanuel Pleitez remembers falling asleep while writing his scholarship essays. In fact, he worked so late, that he went to the post office at the Los Angeles airport to mail his applications because that was the only post office open until midnight. Fortunately, he had a classmate who joined him on these late night drives.

"You have to surround yourself with friends who are motivated like you, who want to go to college and apply for scholarships," he says.

Emanuel and his friend developed an informal support network for each other when applying for awards. He used his friend's computer because he didn't have one and the two helped edit each other's work. In fact, Emanuel encouraged his friend to apply for an award that he found. His friend ultimately won the award.

His classmate wasn't the only person that Emanuel relied on for help. He received encouragement from his coach, who was also his senior class advisor and school's dean. His counselor mentored him after Emanuel approached him during his freshman year of high school to explain his ambition to attend a selective college. He gained interviewing experience at a program he attended to prepare students for internships and essay-writing help from the Quest summer school program he attended at Stanford.

"I was really lucky to be surrounded by all these good people. At every stage there was always a couple of people who I could turn to for help," Emanuel says.

distinguish voices in a noisy room. The hardest part was exhaustion from having to focus on everything going on. School became far harder. Conventional hearing aids don't work with total deafness, so I tried a microphone and receiver system in class. However, it was more frustrating than helpful. After that, my teachers were dazzled with my attentiveness, not realizing I was reading their lips. All this has been very tough emotionally.

With my parents' help I learned not only to cope but to grow. Most people never know I have a severe hearing problem. I turn my head or move so they're on my "good ear" side. I ask people to clarify when statements are unclear. I still play sports, especially lacrosse, though my coach nearly goes hoarse yelling to me.

I challenged myself, joining symphonic band and chamber singers and taking a lead in "The Fantasticks" musical. Enormous hours were spent pinging on the piano, trying to match my voice to notes. The support of friends and teachers was wonderful, and we received rave reviews for the performances.

The struggle has brought me closer to my 90-year-old grandmother, who is losing her hearing. We visit daily and watch PBS together on weekends, the volume blasting. We empathize with each other, laughing and crying over the frustrations of deafness. When volunteering in the hospital cardiac care unit, I comfort older patients by comparing hearing aids. They laugh and do not feel quite so old.

Spring three years ago brought an incredible gift. A doctor developed a trans-cranial hearing aid. It transmits sounds powerfully from the deaf ear, through the skull, to the nerves in the "good" ear. Now, I hear some stereophonic sound and tonality. This cutting edge solution has helped me decide to study engineering, to help others as I have been helped. Engineering is a noble profession; its goal is to alleviate the human condition. I seek to examine and solve problems by creating new visions that combine innovation with technological development.

My invisible handicap makes communication difficult, but I wanted to help other youth grow and develop life skills, faith and values. So, I pushed myself and took increased leadership in Boy Scouts and in my church. These positions require good communication, making me work extremely hard. But the results have been worth the effort. As the leader of the Presbyterian Youth Connection Council for the Synod of the Northeast, I have worked with youth and adults from eight states. We hold training events to improve youth leadership. I went

to Colorado to help the Synod of the Rocky Mountains
establish a youth council. Twice we have planned confer-
ences for nearly 200 youth. I have learned to work until
a task is completed.

Though unable to say I'm glad it happened, I have
benefited from my hearing loss. I have learned to use
my limitations to help others and to never give up. My
no longer monotone voice now reflects the non-monotone
life I have developed.

Nhia TongChai Lee, Knight Ridder Minority Scholar

Nhia comes from a Hmong family where tradition is important.
If his parents had their way, he would never date or even have
friends of the opposite sex. While he respects his parents and his
family's values, he feels that it's important that Hmong of his
generation take steps toward independence and leadership. As
he says, "Just make sure you take big steps and not little baby
steps." And through writing he wants to be someone who influ-
ences those of his generation.

It's because of this desire to inspire others that Nhia got involved
in his newspaper at Lansing Everett High School in Lansing,
Michigan, and is now majoring in journalism at Michigan State
University. His passion to affect others through his writing has
been recognized. He has won over $60,000 in scholarships in-
cluding the Michigan State University Distinguished Freshman
Achievement Award and *Detroit Free Press* Journalism Award.
When asked his planned career field, he says that he will become
the editor of *Rolling Stone*.

Only The Strong Survive

Our lives are not predetermined but rather a journey
that each individual must decide for himself. Events
that transpire along the way do not just disrupt the
journey but sometimes occur to benefit it. During the
Vietnam War, my family was forced out of their home-
land Laos and into Thailand, where they sought refuge for
five years. All was left behind to take a stab at giving
my siblings and me a possible future. The only life they

knew had been wiped clear of existence. The familiar air breathed, land cultivated and faces seen all seemed like a lost dream.

Relocating in Thailand did not manifest into the Promised Land everyone had heard about. Instead of the beautiful lands and abundance of food, what they found were crowded camps and no food. Hunger spread like wildfire and people died by the handful. What many thought was a safe haven was in actuality a waiting deathbed.

Only the strong survived the refugee camps. My family members were just more faces in the crowd of thousands in the same situation. It was there that I was born into a life deprived of the simple good things in life. Finding food was always a problem and just trying to survive to the next day was a top priority. My parents knew that in order to survive we had to leave the refugee camps. If you were lucky, you were sponsored to move to America. Along with thousands of others, we had nothing to do but wait. Wait for a reply to our pleas to leave.

In 1985 my family finally received word that our prayers out of Thailand were answered. A church in Michigan sponsored our family and that was our ticket out. We immigrated to the United States to start anew. We had to adopt a new language, a new culture and a whole new way of life. Through it all, we continued to practice our culture and customs. That was something my parents wanted to keep and pass on to generations to come. It was the only thing about the past that remained with us. My parents wanted us to grow up to be traditional Hmong boys and girls.

I knew what I wanted in life, but knowing that traditionally Hmong children married at a young age, it was hard to break out of that mold. By choosing journalism as a career path, I hope to set an example: following the traditional rules is not the only option, even though that's the only life we know. I want to complete school and have my writing reach a vast audience. I hope to make a difference with writing and show the youth of my culture that we can balance both worlds at the same time. We can still have respect for our parents and compassion for our culture while changing along with modern society. There is a lot more out there for us, a world beyond marriage and children, a world that can show a whole different perspective on life.

I want to show that growing up impoverished can still lead to being published in a national newspaper or writing a Pulitzer Prize-winning article. I want to be that role model for Hmong kids who sometimes feel trapped within the walls that are built around them.

I believe that if I can live my life the way I want it and not how my parents want it, then others can follow. Instead of marrying into a burden-filled life, I can become the anchor for that change. I want to take the path that my parents never spoke of. I know that in the end that will be the difference between what is and what could have been. Hopefully young people, not just Hmong kids, but anyone who feels lost can look at what I have achieved and find their own path.

Jennifer Chiu, Telluride Association Summer Program Scholarship Winner

Jennifer had the opportunity to experience college life while she was still in high school. As a junior at Hunter College High School in New York City, she won a full scholarship to the Telluride Association Summer Program on constitutional law at Cornell University. The program exposes students from a variety of backgrounds to college life and courses. Jennifer used her experience to make the transition to Yale University. In addition to this award, she also won the *New York Times* College Scholarship, National Merit Scholarship and Yale Club of New York City Scholarship. She gives the following advice about applying for awards, "Don't stress too much over sending in the perfect application. Behind every piece of paper is a person, not a robot."

Lessons From A Pitbull

Every time I walked down 52nd Avenue on my way home from the library, I passed a mean pitbull that always barked at and tried to attack strangers. For some reason, he seemed to hate me especially. I suppose that dogs instinctively protect their territory against all intruders and that I qualified. Yet, I was a very poor intruder at best. Whenever I saw him, I cowered next to the hedges, but he would always smell my fear and start his tirade. Perhaps it was my fault for not crossing over to the opposite sidewalk. I didn't want to admit to myself that I was scared.

One afternoon, after having had an especially bad day, I passed him once again. When he started to yap as usual, something snapped inside of me, and I growled back. I think that I could have been heard all the way into the next street. When the dog's owner came out to see what was going on, I ran away.

After that, I avoided the house.

On the surface, the conflict was simple: a struggle for territory. That dog simply did not want me around, while I insisted on it. But deeper down, the problem was my refusal to admit that I was scared of him. My foolish courage rested on the notion that I had a fear of being afraid. I refused to believe that every day is a struggle for survival, since humans have supposedly evolved beyond this. Obviously this is untrue, and now I realize that I, like any other creature, experience terror.

As I battled the dog, I felt conflict with myself at a deeper level. I realized I had a superiority complex, since I was better off in some ways than other people. That would boost my motivation to succeed, but it came at the cost of being alienated and eternally conscious of my weaknesses. I always watched my back, even when it was not necessary. I was intimidated by other people just like I was intimidated even by the dog. I paid the price of needless self-torture and confusion.

This barking episode was one decisive moment in my life. Though it is embarrassing, after all, I proved myself worthy against a dog, not all lessons can be picture-perfect. I'm glad I learned it the hard way than never at all. I realized that I am allowed to admit that I am afraid sometimes, as long as I am willing to work to mediate the anxiety.

Last week, I walked past the house again. It was abandoned and a "For Sale" sign adorned the front yard. I turned on my heels and left.

The Intangible Benefits Of Applying
U.C. Berkeley Scholarship Connection

You have something to gain by applying for scholarships even if you don't win says Leah Carroll, coordinator of U.C. Berkeley's Haas Scholars program and former program coordinator of the university's Scholarship Connection. In her roles Carroll has assisted Berkeley students with applying for awards, especially for the highly competitive scholarships, including the Rhodes, Marshall and Truman.

While Carroll gives students feedback on their essays and practices interviewing them, she reminds them that there is more than scholarship dollars at stake.

"I also emphasize the fringe benefits. For starters you get to know your professors better than before since you need to speak with them," she says. Carroll adds, "You also get practice presenting yourself in interviews and on paper." This is helpful for students who will soon be applying for jobs or for graduate school. She says that the essays can even serve as rough drafts of graduate school admission essays.

And looking at the big picture, Carroll says that applying for one of these awards "forces you to analyze your own life." She says that one of the things she enjoys most about her job is helping students clarify their purpose in life through the process of applying for scholarships.

Essays About Family

Rodolfo Valadez, Cohen Foundation Scholarship Winner

Going to Thomas Jefferson High School in Los Angeles, California, Rodolfo discovered his passion: filmmaking. While making movies including his critically acclaimed documentary "los angeles," which was screened at the Sundance Film Festival, is his passion, Rodolfo's inspiration is his mother. Rodolfo freely admits that his mother is "my support, my help, my guidance, my friend, my hero." With this essay, Rodolfo won a $6,000 scholarship from the Cohen Foundation and $7,000 scholarship from the Hispanic Heritage Youth Awards to attend the University of California at Los Angeles.

A Mother's Sacrifice

My mother sat in between the dry grass growing out of the puddle of dirt water under a bridge in the hills separating Mexico from San Diego. In that exact moment I sat aboard a plane with strangers and in possession of a name other than mine in order to be granted admission into the United States. It has now been 14 years, and my mother still sacrifices her own comfort for mine. She works nine hours a day, six days a week in a machine-like position, humped over a sewing machine, altering clothes for strangers. At the same time I sit in class, socializing, enjoying a productive school day.

However, my mother is fulfilled knowing that her children take advantage of the vast opportunities this country has to offer despite the hardships she has to endure for a weekly paycheck. A paycheck she has vowed to invest into my college education at UCLA, an institution requiring almost $16,000 a year. At her hourly salary and after taxes she would have to work 2,560 hours in order to pay a year's tuition, which equals working 10,240 hours over the four years of college. If asked to, she would be more than willing to undergo the task of paying for my education knowing fully the standards and strife she would burden herself with.

In my sophomore year, I was among 24 honor students sequestered into a film course. I became one of the first students to attend the annual Telluride Film Festival in Colorado. In my second year in the course I attended the Sundance Film Festival where I was able to display my own work. Again, in my final year, we were invited to Sundance to show more films from our Academy of Film and Theatre Arts.

The film I showcased in the student forum was a documentary film commemorating my mother's struggle and sacrifice ever since her departure from a small oasis named Los Angeles in Durango, Mexico, only to move into the cold, industrial city of Los Angeles, California. The film depicts her struggle and reason for doing so. It also illuminates the fact that more like her exist all around us.

The film course at my high school has been my passion. For three years the course taught me to acquire a more perceptive and critical view of the world. Throughout the course we studied Aristotle's philosophies and the evolution of cinematography, and we analyzed films and wrote essays comparing the motifs they translate into a sequence of shots. I have become more creative and just recently started working on a new 16 mm film entitled "Love Story." As clichéd as the title suggests, the story is a satire of what the title represents. Such projects motivate me to work even when class is over. In the last three years I have found myself in class Saturday mornings and afternoons, editing and brainstorming ideas with classmates.

I have my mother to thank for being able to pursue my passion in filmmaking. I realize she gave up everything for me, and I will do what I can to make it well worth it.

Jessica Haskins, SuperCollege.com Scholarship Winner

Jessica's dream is to write fantasy novels and short stories. Throughout her time at Saratoga Springs High School in Saratoga Springs, New York, Jessica took challenging classes and focused on obtaining a wide breadth of knowledge that would be useful in her future career. She is studying creative writing at Bard College. Outside of classes, she keeps up her writing with day and dream journals. When writing her essay, Jessica had a difficult time with the length requirement. "Editing is terrible," she admits, but after much cutting she was able to pare down her essay to meet the requirements. Although Jessica was worried that her essay had lost much of its power, her editors assured her that it had not. Obviously, the judges concurred.

Thank You, Dr. Seuss

(With Special Recognition for the Trenton, Georgia, School System)

More than anything else I can think up as a reason, my mother is why I'm going to college. Because of her, there could be no other decision. Not that I'm being forced or anything, but she has heavily influenced me and my decision. In a good way.

She always regretted that she could never go to college. Her parents, her teachers and her school counselors somehow, even though I still have trouble understanding it, simply never arranged it for her. College has always been a foregone conclusion for me, so this seems bizarre. To this day, she's never been able to explain it to my satisfaction. Nor to her own.

My mother is a very intelligent woman and was one of the best students in her small-town, athletics-minded Georgia high school (3rd or so in her class, where rank was unweighted and the valedictorian did as little as she could to get 100's in easy classes). She's certain that she could have accomplished a lot in life if she'd only been able to get a college education. She swears her education actually stopped at 9th grade, when she moved from Illinois to Georgia. I've seen the white sticker she uses as a bookmark in her gigantic Random House Dictionary of the English Language. It says "I [heart] Georgia," with the heart crossed out in black marker. She does love things like warm weather, big flowers and Southern cooking but despises their educational system.

I grew up knowing how keenly she lamented her missed opportunity, and she passed on her appreciation for the value of education to me. From the start she raised me to be an intellectual. I could read by age 3. I have a vivid memory of lying on the couch with her in the living room of our old house right on Route 9, where the cars would streak past day and night. My mother was reading Dr. Seuss to me--"We run for fun in the hot, hot sun," from *One Fish, Two Fish, Red Fish, Blue Fish*--and afternoon sunlight was pouring in through the windows, warming the whole room. As she read, I followed along. That was my first memory of ever actually reading the words, rather than just being read to. Whenever I think of my educational success, I attribute it first and foremost to learning to read at an early age, and the very next thing I think of is that reading lesson in the sun.

I have another memory. Me, at about the same age, confronting my father in the bathroom and asking, "Daddy, when can I go to school?" I just couldn't wait. I went to two years of preschool, where I did very well, except that I wasn't very generous. Recently I was poking through my old school files and found a couple of reports from one of my preschools. In fact, let me go get them so that I can quote it exactly--ah, here it is. "Jessica needs prompting to share." I found that very amusing. Now that I think about it, I was pretty attached to that Viewmaster.

When I was finally old enough I went to kindergarten, but nothing there was a challenge for me, and my parents and I all wanted me to skip a grade. It took a little battling with the school, which was reluctant to move me ahead, and some extensive testing, but they finally agreed to have me skip first grade. I'm glad that I did. Even though I was younger than the other kids in my grade, I took advanced classes whenever there was an opportunity. Because of the importance my mother always placed on education, I was always ready to take on harder material.

As I said before, it was always a given that I would go to college. My mother wanted it for me, and I wanted it for myself. And not just any college--my aim was never to just get a degree and a good job, but to

continue to enrich myself. The "good job" isn't even
guaranteed. After all, I want to be a writer, and
there's no ticket to success in that field without a
good bit of luck. So my standards for college are
slightly different. Basically what I want is the most
liberal of liberal arts. I want to continue the educational path that started way back when I was lying on
the living room couch reading *One Fish, Two Fish, Red
Fish, Blue Fish* with my mother, who knew I'd someday
get the college experience she never had. So thank you,
Dr. Seuss. And thank you, Mom.

Donald H. Matsuda, Jr., Truman Scholarship Winner

Working as an intern for a health clinic, Donald read an article in
the *New York Times*. The headline was, "Forty-four Million Americans Without Health Insurance." When he learned through the
article that over one-third of these Americans were children, he
decided to take action. With the help of the clinic's director, he
secured the funding for and developed a series of insurance drives
for Asian immigrant children. In addition to his work with the
clinic, Donald is the founder of the San Mateo Children's Health
Insurance Program, the national director of United Students for
Veterans' Health and the founder of the Nepal Pediatric Clinical
Internship.

A Stanford University student from Sacramento, California, where
he attended Jesuit High School, Donald plans to use the $30,000
Truman Scholarship to obtain a medical degree and master's degree in public administration and would eventually like to be the
medical director of a nonprofit clinic to aid underserved popula-
tions and the uninsured.

When Drinking Water

When drinking water, my grandmother would often proclaim, "Never forget its source." For some reason, I
always enjoyed hearing her repeat these words of
wisdom from her book of ancient Asian proverbs. Perhaps it was because I had grown to fully appreciate
its true meaning--that one must always remember and
treasure their ancestry and elders, who are viewed as the

ultimate source of life. Or, perhaps it was because I felt this proverb effectively expressed my own sentiments about my life.

Growing up as an only child, I developed a very close relationship with my entire family and I greatly valued the time I was able to spend in the company of my elders, especially my grandmother. As a survivor of the Japanese American internment camps, she maintained an unbridled idealism, an impeccable work ethic and a genuine compassion for those in need. Moreover, she was intent on instilling these values in me when I was a young boy. I often looked to her as my true source of strength, for she always infused me with energy, passion and ideals.

Two years ago, I received a call from my parents urging me to return home. When I got there, I saw my mother was on the verge of tears as she told me what was wrong: "Grandma passed away today. She had a massive stroke and the doctors did everything they could, but..." I embraced my mother and we cried for what seemed like an eternity. I soon realized that I had lost not only my grandmother, but also a precious source of inspiration and strength.

Since that tragic day, I have become a much stronger person. I have internalized grandma's work ethic, idealism and compassion so that my source of strength now comes from within. It is this new motivation that fuels my convictions and drives my passion for a life dedicated to public service.

Every day, when I pass by the elegantly sculpted water fountains on my way to class, I pause as cherished memories of my grandmother fill my mind, and I know in my heart that I will never forget my true source.

Chheng Sok, Chicago Scholars Foundation Winner

Every time Chheng announced good news to her parents, they gave her their special smile. Her parents grew up in Cambodia, where her father's education ended in grade school and her mother did not receive a formal education. So it held special meaning when Chheng was accepted to the University of Chicago. She received her parents' special smile. And when she won over $35,000 in scholarships, their smile broadened even wider.

Graduating from Lane Technical School in Chicago, Chheng was president of the Chinese Club and involved in public service. She encourages others to apply for scholarships. As she says, "I'm not exactly the best student, but I still got scholarships." Majoring in East Asian Language and Civilization and Economics at the University of Chicago, she plans a career in education or international business.

My Family's Hope

My family and I immigrated to the United States from Cambodia to flee the ravages of the Khmer Rouge when I was only a year old. We did not have a single penny when we came to the United States. I remember seeing my father diligently collect soda cans on the streets to trade in to the local recycling center for a penny each. I remember watching my family silently endure the rudeness of waiters and salespeople because we did not speak grammatically correct English and realizing at the age of five how much illiteracy paralyzes a person.

I am the youngest out of my parent's nine children, yet I possess the greatest amount of education. My father can barely read English. My mother is totally illiterate. Due to my family's financial situation, none of my eight siblings have completed college. Throughout my elementary and high school years, I oftentimes had difficulty with my schoolwork. I remember staying up late at night, sometimes until two in the morning, just so that I could figure out the answer to a homework problem. My parents and older siblings, as much as they wanted to help me on my assignments, were unable to because they simply did not understand the material. They would quietly sit by me and bring me refreshments from time to time and offer me encouragement. My siblings make me realize how priceless knowledge is and to make the most out of one's education.

My parents look at me as my family's hope for the future. They dream that I will some day graduate from an American university. They want to be able to send back letters to our relatives in China and in Cambodia, telling them about how one person in the family has gained an American diploma. I want to be the realization of their dream and my dream. I dream of graduating from one of the finest colleges in America, the University of Chicago. I hope that someday I will be able to repay my parents for all the years they have lovingly supported me. I want to be able to financially and intellectually provide for my family so that we no longer have to endure the discrimination toward illiteracy.

In addition, I strive to succeed in school because I want to be a role model for my nieces and nephews. As a student, I personally know how tough it can be to excel in school. I want to be there to help them if they need help on a class assignment, to guide them through their first multiplication table and to be their mentor when they start the college selection process.

With knowledge, one need not fear being cheated by a salesman or being looked down upon by an egotistical snob. Education is the door that opens the path to knowledge. With knowledge, I am in control of my life and my destiny.

National Or International Issues

Elizabeth Ashlea Wood, Optimist International Essay Contest Winner

After having witnessed a nuclear disaster, Elizabeth knew that her life was changed. She says, "It really opened my eyes. It got me away from thinking that I'm young and can live forever." Touched, she wrote about the experience for this award to share her fear and realizations with others. A graduate of the Classen School of Advanced Studies for Performing and Visual Arts in Oklahoma City, she is studying literature, writing and the arts at Eugene Lang College in New York City.

The Tokai Nuclear Disaster

Last year on an October evening in Japan, I enjoyed the rain, walking slowly to my host family's farm for the night. After I yelled the customary "Tadaima" and removed my shoes my host mother pulled out a heavy English dictionary. She searched for a word and then pointed excitedly. Above her finger I read "radiation." The Tokai nuclear power plant two miles away was experiencing a severe accident. Soon trucks driving by screamed warnings in Japanese to prepare for nuclear disaster. My body was numb.

I had been to Hiroshima the week before. All I could imagine were the grotesque pictures of goiters and dripping flesh. Photographs of the burnt remains of an ancient city flashed in my head. I remembered seeing the "Daisy Girl" commercial from LBJ's presidential campaign in government class. It slowly played in my mind, a blonde child holding a daisy, framed by a green-gray mushroom cloud. My imagination forced me to expect the worst.

The air terrified me. I thought I was suffocating. In that moment I could not understand how my life had led to this crucial moment. I had left my home for a beautiful opportunity to live in Japan and experience the culture. I had joined an exchange program in a small

Essay Advice From The Winners
Scholarship Winners

Here are some essay tips from scholarship winners. Having survived various competitions these winners have a unique understanding of what goes into crafting a winning essay.—Gen & Kelly

Donald H. Matsuda, Jr.
Stanford University student and Truman Scholar
"If readers can connect with you, feel your emotions and feel they know you, that you're such a dynamic person, that comes across in your writing. That really is a plus. You can espouse all the pros and cons of think tanks in the American political system but that doesn't really help the committee learn who you are."

Dalia Alcázar
U.C. Berkeley student and scholarship winner
"Your essays are the most time consuming part of applying. Some of the questions are very similar. You might have a couple essays already written that you can modify. For many of the scholarships I won I used the same essay with slight modifications."

Sara Bei
Stanford University student and scholarship winner
"Sometimes the ones you end up winning are the ones you almost didn't apply for. Even if it takes a long time to fill out applications and write essays, think of it as being paid $500 an hour if you win."

Jessica Haskins
Bard College student and scholarship winner
"The topic doesn't have to be profound. You don't have to write about the time you saved someone's life, or describe an earth-shattering experience—I personally think that a simple, thoughtful and honest reflection carries more weight than an elevated epic of love, loss and life's lessons in 500 words or less."

Jason Morimoto
U.C. Berkeley student and scholarship winner
"Use your essay to craft a story showing why you are a unique candidate. Include personal experiences, lessons learned and how you are trying to improve yourself."

village by the ocean. This succession of serendipitous events led me to the only place in the entire world where a severe nuclear disaster was occurring. My choices had exposed me to the ultimate weapon of our time; I was waiting for radiation to subside. The rice paper windows and layers of silk robes provided little comfort. There was nothing I could do to protect myself from the danger. In that moment I could only learn.

The world's issues no longer can disappear as I close a schoolbook. On that autumn evening I was suddenly a part of one of the nemeses of the twentieth century: nuclear energy. Ironically, my frightening experience was only an accident. When I decided to embrace a three-month adventure I never expected to trade in theater and friends for a serious nuclear disaster. My eyes were pried open to make me realize that the world's issues are not separate from my American life. I realized that I had been educated about the world to understand cause and effects, the cycles of history and of the future, but I had not metacognitively incorporated them into a worldview.

That evening reached into my mind and opened a door to the realities of this world. The Tokai disaster threatened my life, but it also demonstrated the capabilities for any person to experience the same shocking circumstances. In Japan, quarantined for days on a Buddhist farm, I could see no separation of myself from other cultures. I realized that I could no longer segregate America from other countries, my race from other races, Oklahoma from Japan. Three days after the Tokai nuclear disaster I stepped out of the farmhouse into the fresh sunshine of a glorious oriental garden. Over a cup of green tea I determined to be committed to my new perception of the world as an entirety.

Elisa Tatiana Juárez, Target All-Around Scholarship Winner

Based on her research in osteoporosis and gerontology, Elisa has placed first and best in show in a number of science competitions including the Intel International Science and Engineering Fair and the South Florida Science and Engineering Fair. But each time she entered a science competition, she noticed that economically disadvantaged students were underrepresented. She did something to change this. Working with the Miami Museum of Science and Big Brothers Big Sisters of Greater Miami, she founded the Students and Teachers Advocating Research Science (STARS) program to provide assistance to economically-disadvantaged middle school children.

In addition to STARS, Elisa has been recognized by the United States Air Force for her research in gerontology and was selected to present her work to the Florida state legislature for her research on osteoporosis. Her commitment to the sciences has paid off. She has won scholarships including the National Hispanic Heritage Youth Award for Science and Technology and the Science Silver Knight Award. A graduate of Coral Reef Senior High School in Miami, she is a student at Brown University.

STARS

I developed the STARS (Students and Teachers Advocating Research Science) Project to provide information, materials, and, most importantly, mentors, to help middle school students from at-risk environments to complete and present successful science projects. STARS now helps the Miami Museum of Science and Big Brothers Big Sisters of Greater Miami to "support and empower single-parent families to actively engage in their children's science education."

STARS grew as an extension of my own involvement with science research projects that have been successful at local, regional, state and international levels. I had a lot of support from family, teachers and mentors and wanted to find a way to offer similar support and opportunities for students who didn't have all that. American students are losing ground internationally in science and math, and I wanted to find a way to share my passion in tangible ways.

Why science? I feel that it is important for every kid to be involved in science. The Third International Mathematics and Science Study (TIMSS) showed that U.S.

12th graders outperformed only two (Cyprus and South Africa) of the 21 participating countries in math and science. All kids need to have access to better opportunities in science, and this project has allowed kids who had never even thought about science research to discover that they can do anything they want to do.

I think the most memorable part of this project was to see the kids' eyes sparkle when they talked about their ideas for projects and then began to see the results of actually doing the research. I remember at the end of a workshop, one of the girls came up to me and said that she really enjoyed the day. I asked her what she meant, and she said with a smile, "Well, I don't really do science. I'm more into English and literature. When I heard about this, I didn't really want to come, but I am so glad I did. I had so much fun learning that I could do a good project. I think my teacher will be proud."

I am now designing a STARS science curriculum that correlates with the National Science Education Standards. I hope that Big Brothers Big Sisters chapters around the country will be able to use the curriculum to encourage their "littles" and "bigs" to participate more actively in science.

Based on this experience so far, I would tell other young people that there is nothing more rewarding than realizing that you can make a difference. That you can identify a need, develop a solution, find people to help you accomplish your goals. Of course, I would also tell them that science is everywhere and is exciting and can help you learn about the universe and about yourself.

Elisa Tatiana Juárez, Presbyterian Church USA Scholarship Winner

The Power To Change The World

When people ask me what I want to do when I grow up, I answer them quite simply and firmly, "I am going to

change the world." I am 17 years old, but I have known
for a very long time that I would, in some way, be
responsible for shaping the world of the future.
Crazy? Maybe. Impossible? Definitely not.

Unfortunately, in my experience, it has been kids my
age who tell me that I am just a dreamer and that there
is no way I could possibly make a difference in the
world. "Come on Elisa," they tell me, "You're just a kid.
No one in his or her right mind is going to listen to
some high school girl. Don't bother; no one cares anyway.
Someone else will do it."

I think that the greatest opportunity facing youth
today is the power to better the world around us by
using new tools, new technologies and a new understanding of the global community. By the same token I
believe that the most urgent problem facing youth
today is indifference. The general attitude about
everything and anything is "Who cares? I am not that
important, there is nothing I can do about it." I find
this incredibly sad and distressing. God gives us the
intelligence to build the tools; we only need to use
them with the guidance of His Spirit guided by His
love.

My generation is very cynical when it comes to helping
out. They claim that what they have to say couldn't
possibly be important enough to be heard by others.
What they don't understand are two very important
concepts. First of all, the majority of the youth
today don't realize that there are plenty of problems
in their own community. Making a difference doesn't
always mean moving to Somalia to end hunger. It could
mean something along the lines of helping a migrant
family learn the basics of the English language.
Second of all, youth today don't realize how something
very simple can change someone's entire world. By
teaching that family English, for example, they will
feel more comfortable in this country.

Growing up I heard a story about an old man who goes
down to the sea one morning. He notices that a young
girl is reaching down and throwing starfish into the
water. Curious, he walks over to the girl and asks her

what she is doing. She replies, "Well, the tide is awfully low, and if I don't throw the starfish into the water the sun will dry them out." The old man looked at her and laughed. There were miles of shore with thousands of starfish. The little girl couldn't possibly throw all the starfish back in the sea. He told her she wouldn't be able to make a difference. The little girl bent down scooping up yet another starfish. She turned it over in her hand processing what the man had told her. Then, looking at the old man, she placed the starfish in his hands and helped him throw it back into the sea and moved on to the next starfish. She looked over her shoulder and said, "Well, to that starfish, I made a world of difference."

This is where the story traditionally ends. I have added on to it. The man, realizing the power this little girl had over the lives of the starfish, called up his grandchildren. Together they worked at saving the stranded starfish. That day, maybe not all the starfish were saved, but those that were, I'm sure, were very grateful. They continued living because of the determination of a little girl who knew that she could make a difference and could find ways to get others involved.

We must each find our starfish. If we throw our stars wisely and well, the world will be blessed. I constantly am praying for the strength to carry on and for the courage to help others find the power within them to help shape the world of today.

Shashank Bengali, Scripps-Howard College Journalism Scholarship Winner

Shashank knew that his parents wouldn't be able to foot the entire bill for his education at a private college, especially since his younger brother would soon follow him to college. Rather than look for a less-expensive school, Shashank decided to take action by applying for scholarships. His advisers at Whitney High School in Cerritos, California, suggested that he apply for the awards for which he would be the best candidate. Journalism awards were a natural fit.

Since the age of 13, Shashank has worked for his school newspaper. As the editor, he won a national competition for the Knight Ridder Minority Journalism Scholarship, which allowed him to intern at four newspapers across the country while in school. In addition, he won a full-tuition scholarship from the University of Southern California and Scripps-Howard College Journalism Scholarship, awarded to 10 college journalists in the country. He recently graduated with a degree in broadcast journalism, political science and French and is working as a Missouri state correspondent for *The Kansas City Star.*

Media Misunderstandings

On the day of the New Hampshire primary this year, the online magazine Slate.com posted early exit-poll results on its site before voting had closed for the day, inciting an enormous outcry in the traditional media. The major newspapers and television networks, bound by contract to honor an embargo on those results, said Slate violated the law--and a journalistic trust with the people. Slate disagreed, and went ahead publishing exit-poll results on the days of several other primaries this season, before being threatened with a lawsuit.

On the question of law, at least, Slate never agreed to any embargo. The other question, of the people's trust, is murkier, because it's unclear whether knowing preliminary election results actually deters voters from going to the polls. Tempers ran high on both sides here, with Slate columnist Jack Schafer going so far as to write in a Wall Street Journal op-ed piece that the Big Three networks' coverage of primary results is "all an act."

I bring up this story to illustrate a point: the relationship between "old" and "new" media is in real disrepair. Finger-pointing and mutual misunderstanding rule the day, when diverse news organizations hardly seem, most times, to understand each other's roles. The fact is, there are now three ways to disseminate information in the world--in print, in broadcast and online. All three have merit, and all three, in some form or another, appear to be here to stay.

What's needed, then, is greater cooperation and less co-optation. If, as many believe, the best news organizations of the near future will be those that are diversified and bring elements of print, broadcast and online media to bear together on their coverage, those journalists who are trained in each form will be the most valuable. I subscribe to this view and I will be one of those "hybrid" journalists, helping guide a shift to more complete, convergent news coverage that encompasses the three forms because I know the power of each.

I consider myself lucky to be around for the old media-new media debate because it's a vital one. I believe that much of the disdain on both sides is a product of misconceptions--and a lack of experience. My generation's position is unique: I've grown up with 24-hour news channels and the Internet, so I know their immediacy and reach in a visceral way. But the reason I got into journalism in the first place was that I love the written word and the prudence of print media. I know that people will always need their daily newspaper and their weekly newsmagazine, no matter how quickly TV and websites can give them their fix.

So I've explored all three realms of journalism during my time in college, and I've discovered that I'm a journalist first and foremost, gladly unfettered by any other labels. Internships at newspapers have reinforced my newsgathering and writing skills. My time as executive producer of USC's nightly newscast has taught me that "print values" can be tuned for broadcast--for visual impact and swift, assured responses to breaking-news situations. And each time a distant friend or relative e-mails me to say they saw our webcast and have feedback, or (better yet) to offer story ideas from their part of the world, I learn the power of the Internet as a medium of news.

Good journalism can be done with these three modes working in concert, but the best journalism can only come with responsible and well-trained leaders at the top, who know how to direct multifaceted coverage because they believe in it and have done it before. That's what I want to do and am learning how to do--help lead the new wave.

I would encourage the sort of synergy that Tribune is pursuing—and that reporters at CNN practice daily when they submit their stories for that network's TV, radio and online products. There is no reason consumers shouldn't have the benefit of the fullest possible picture in a news story; after all, it's what we should strive to give them each time around. Already, on a small scale, I am working to achieve that convergence on our campus. Next year, our newscast and the student newspaper--two entirely distinct organizations--will team up for one in-depth story. We will each pursue the angles to that story that are best suited to our particular medium--visual stories for TV, for example, and longer analysis pieces for print--and we'll use our websites to complete the coverage, including any long documents or transcripts of interviews that can't fit newshole or airtime.

A news organization should be dedicated to the kind of public service in journalism that may uproot the company's tradition for the sake of its work. It makes good business sense, because through responsible convergence you can reach more people with greater speed than your competition. But most important, it improves the product--and that is good journalism.

Of course, I don't know exactly how I'm going to get to a position where I can help implement this vision I share. One thing that's certain about this changing market is that nothing's certain. For the time being, after graduating college, I plan to write for a newspaper--because that's my first love, and still the traditional journalist's ground zero. That's a personal bias, I admit, but my experience in the other realms will probably make me a better print reporter. From that first job to wherever I end up, it's a yet-to-be-paved road. But I am confident in the future of journalism in this new era, and I'll remain dedicated to it.

Lindsay Hyde, National React Take Action Award & Toyota Scholar Winner

When her grandmother received a corneal transplant that saved her vision, it motivated Lindsay to insure that others were educated about the benefits of organ donation. From this single experience the Organ Donor Project was born.

Over three years, the Miami student secured corporate sponsorships to produce an educational curriculum and informational video for other students to view and create their own organ donation awareness programs. The project expanded from Lindsay's own high school, Southwest Miami High School, to 12 schools across the nation and five in Malaysia, Australia, Costa Rica and the United Kingdom.

As a result of her efforts, Lindsay won a number of scholarships including being a National Coca-Cola Scholar, National Toyota Scholar and National React Take Action Award winner. At Harvard University, she is studying sociology and women's studies as well as continuing her volunteer work as the founder of Strong Women, Strong Girls, designed to assist at-risk elementary school girls.

Organ Donor Project

Imagine a stadium filled with 100,000 football fans. The stadium would overflow with people, the sound of cheering would be deafening. Now, imagine the game has finished, but the fans are unable to leave. Instead they sit waiting, waiting for...the unknown. By next year, experts estimate that 100,000 people will be waiting for life-saving organ transplants.

For several months, my grandmother was a fan in that stadium, waiting for a sight-saving corneal transplant. My grandmother was fortunate to receive her transplant, thanks to the generosity of individuals who made the decision to become organ donors.

As a result of my grandmother's experience, I realized the importance of organ donation and the need for accurate organ donation education. To meet this need, I developed a community service project during my sophomore year to provide teenagers with accurate organ donation information. The Organ Donor Project was introduced with a three-day awareness event that included a pep rally, speakers day and fundraising paintball tournament. Over 700 teachers and students

Community Service & Volunteerism

Vanessa Deanne Perplies, Target All-Around Scholarship Winner

As a volunteer for the Los Angeles Police Department Explorer Scout Program, Vanessa has assisted with crime prevention surveillance, evidence searches and police ride alongs. She volunteered nearly 400 hours with the program designed for students who are interested in law enforcement and community service. Her work was one of the reasons she won the Target All-Around Scholarship, which is based on community service. In addition to volunteering with the Explorer Scout Program, Vanessa also raised funds and walked with the North Hollywood High School Zoo Magnet AIDS team and volunteered for Project Chicken Soup preparing and delivering food to AIDS patients. A student at U.C. Santa Barbara, she is majoring in sociology and plans to become either a sociologist or journalist.

Serving & Protecting

One Sunday morning, bright and early, approximately 25 Girl Scouts arrived for a tour of the Los Angeles Police Department Foothill Police Station.

As a Los Angeles Police Department Explorer Scout, it was my task to help these girls. Experiences like this one have shaped and solidified my career goals, in addition to benefiting the children of Los Angeles.

The girls, ranging in ages from 4 to 11, had not only an enjoyable adventure but also learned about important issues such as 911, acting in emergencies and overall safety. I helped the girls try on riot gear, turn on the lights and sirens of police cars and use the police radios. I escorted them through empty jail cells, reminding them of the dangers of the world and teaching them to stay safe.

For young girls who are rarely taught self-reliance, this experience taught them how to take care of themselves. I

was keeping people safe as well as helping them grow up
to be stronger, wiser women. I could see their delight
and curiosity at the unfamiliar environment of a police
station, and I was happy to demystify law enforcement in
such a positive manner.

The gratitude of the little girls showed me the simple
appreciation in a child's smile was a priceless feeling.
The Girl Scouts were not the only ones who learned; I
realized that the things that make me happiest also make
others happy. I have been inspired and challenged to
learn and do more, and especially to reach out and share
the knowledge I can, changing the lives of others for the
better.

Svati Singla, Discover Card Tribute Award Scholarship Winner

Svati says that she has never let society's perception of age stop
her. This was one of the factors that led her to publish an abstract
in the American Journal of Hypertension after years of research–
at the age of 11. Throughout junior high and high school, she
continued her research at East Carolina University on fetal alcohol syndrome, won accolades from the U.S. Navy and Army for
her research and spent three years shadowing surgeons at East
Carolina University Health Systems.

After graduating from J.H. Rose High School in Greenville, North
Carolina, Svati is studying biology with a concentration in genet-
ics at Duke University. She has won an extraordinary $1 million
in scholarships including the Discover Card Gold Tribute Award,
Benjamin N. Duke Leadership Scholarship, Boy Scouts of America National Scholarship and National Merit Scholarship. After
graduating, she plans to attend medical school.

Giving Back To My Community

I dedicate many hours of my time to significant community
service activities. Through my participation in such
service projects and activities, I have learned many
valuable lessons about the significance of each individual in the community.

As a literacy volunteer, I am given the opportunity to see the glow on a mother's face when she realizes that her son will finally be given the gift of the ability to read. I am given the satisfaction of knowing that my time is positively contributing to another's life.

Another community service activity that has significantly influenced the community is my involvement in Teen Court. Teen Court is an alternative program to the court system that provides graduated penalties for juvenile offenders. It is an innovative program that benefits teens on both sides of the court system. The teens who are brought before the Teen Court learn to accept the consequences of their actions, without having a flaw in their permanent record. On the other hand, the teens that comprise the court system are educated about the justice system while they work together for awareness and compliance with the law. As a member of the Teen Court program, I am able to provide far-reaching benefits for all members of the community by keeping the youth well disciplined and well educated.

Recognizing the need for volunteers at a facility for mentally retarded children, I immediately seized the opportunity to make a difference in the lives of these children. As I read and play with them, I realize how simple pleasures bring so much satisfaction and joy to their hearts. I take great pride, knowing that I am spreading a feeling of warmth and happiness with my actions. At the local Boy's and Girl's Club, I have initiated a program, called "Bookworm", which encourages young children to read. As I go and read to these children, I realize that I am not only increasing their interest in reading, but that I am also serving as a role model to them. The children are all motivated to learn and make great strides in their reading. Their interest in education creates a positive attitude towards learning that is beneficial to the community.

As I volunteer for other organizations such as the Salvation Army, American Cancer Society, Knights of Columbus, Greenville Community Shelter, East Carolina University Health Systems and more, I realize how my actions can be compared to a pebble in a pond. Despite the size of the pebble, once it is thrown into the pond, the entire pond feels the pebble's impact through the ripples. Similarly, though I am just one individual in a large community, I am able to make a difference. Dedicated to community service, I am the pebble in the pond.

Donald H. Matsuda, Jr., Truman Scholarship Winner

Camp ReCreation

Working with mentally and physically disabled children over the past four summers has been one of the most amazing and rewarding experiences of my undergraduate career. Before volunteering with Camp ReCreation for Disabled Kids, I shied away from any interaction with the disabled community and remained distant from this group of people whose lives and problems seemed so very different from my own. Nevertheless, I felt compelled to bridge this gap, and I decided to board the bus for my first experience at Camp ReCreation.

During this first summer, I took care of a deaf boy named Michael. At first, I was quite frustrated because I was unable to establish any means of communication with him. However, I did not see this problem as an insurmountable obstacle; instead, I viewed it as a challenge that could be overcome with some dedication and perseverance on my part. Over the next week, I voraciously read all books I could find on sign language, and I devoted most of my nights to mastering this very complex form of communication. My tireless efforts paid off, as Michael began to recognize my signs and responded with frequent smiles, indicating his understanding and acceptance. As Michael began to open up and even sign back, I realized that we had developed a special and meaningful relationship--one that provided him with happiness and one that solidified my genuine love of service.

I eagerly returned to camp for three more summers. One summer I worked with Nick, a mildly autistic teenager to improve his communication skills. Last year, I helped Brittney, a young girl with a neurological disorder, in developing better motor coordination. Despite the differing needs of each camper, I still maintained the camp's

mission: to provide a positive and healthy summer experience for disabled youth. In return, I gained the love and
friendship of disabled kids and learned that these children have needs that are not unlike my own. I truly value
my Camp ReCreation experience because it has fueled my
passion to protect and promote the rights of children
nationwide.

Emily Kendall, Association For Women In Science Scholarship Winner

To tutor a struggling math student, Emily drew on the patience
that her own teachers had shown her when she was younger. This
is the topic of Emily's essay, which she wrote to win a number of
scholarships and to apply to Harvard, Duke, MIT, Washington
University in St. Louis, Caltech, Vanderbilt and the University of
Chicago. In fact, she not only gained admission to all but also
received a number of offers of full scholarships. In addition to
her volunteer work, she has been named a national semifinalist
in both the Intel and Siemens-Westinghouse national science research competitions, led her high school academic team to two
state championships and been one of two delegates from her state
to participate in the U.S. Senate Youth Program. A graduate of
North High School in Evansville, Indiana, she is now studying
physics at Harvard University.

A Lesson For Both Of Us

June pursed her lips and furrowed her brow as I
plunged into yet another problem demonstrating least
common denominators. Recognizing June's confusion and
exasperation, I wracked my brain for a simpler approach, but as I spoke, the blank expression on June's
face foretold my impending failure. I waited hopefully
as she puzzled over the final step, but she dropped
her pencil and sighed, "Negative numbers just don't
make sense!"

Clearly, June was frustrated. So was I. All my life, I
had ceaselessly soaked up knowledge from books and asked
questions about everything around me. I explored new
ideas; I pushed myself to achieve and to learn far more

than my classes required; and when it came to math, I
would gladly spend days pondering a challenging problem.
Why couldn't this girl be more like I am? Or at least
more like my other pupils? My other math students studied
faithfully; my freshman debaters shared insightful new
arguments with me daily; even little Hernando, whom I
tutored in inner-city Chicago, had been thrilled to have
a friend who would study with him.

Part of me wanted to give up on June, but then I realized
that some of my own difficult experiences, which had
shaped me greatly, could help me to help June. I recalled
my painful rejection from the first grade "select choir."
That experience, although it had taught me to accept
failures with grace and learn from them, had still hurt
terribly, so I resolved never to let anyone label June a
failure at math. I also recalled my determination to make
the eighth grade volleyball team and the countless hours
I spent lifting weights and repeatedly serving the volleyball alone in my backyard before I earned a school
uniform. Recognizing the persistence necessary to achieve
something difficult, I determined to work my hardest
until June mastered her algebra. Finally, I recalled
my enthusiastic middle school teacher whose coaching
helped and inspired me to win local MATHCOUNTS competitions, qualify for the state team and advance with
my teammates to place second nationally. Seeing the
value of a committed, motivated, enthusiastic teacher
who puts more faith in you than you put in yourself, I
promised myself that, despite my frustration, I would
not give up on my student.

As I move on to college and beyond, I intend to excel,
but more importantly, I want my endeavors to have a
positive influence on others. As I work toward this end,
I am thankful for my talents and my successes; however, I
recognize that some of the greatest gifts I can offer are
the perseverance, humility, compassion or strength aris-
ing from apparent defeat. Drawing on my natural abilities
and life's lessons, I can continue to help others as I
helped June, whose blank looks turned to expressions of
understanding, whose signs of frustration became promising smiles and who, though I still have much to teach
her, finally believes she can succeed.

Career Plans Or Field Of Study

Danny Fortson, Rotary International Ambassadorial Scholarship Winner

Danny applied for the Rotary scholarship as a way of not only studying journalism but also doing so abroad. He will use the award to gain formal training in journalism and to continue his studies in Spanish. A graduate of U.C. Santa Barbara, Danny's experiences include writing for two San Francisco-based publications, studying abroad in Costa Rica and interning for the Center for Strategic and International Studies, a foreign policy think tank. He thinks he won the award because of his persistence. An unsuccessful applicant the previous year, he used the time in between to increase his qualifications with more journalism experience which is clearly evident in his essay.

International Journalism

Several months ago, I walked into the local bicycle shop, picked out one of the few two-wheelers that fit my lanky frame, strapped a Styrofoam helmet to my head, and set about riding my bike to work every day through the hectic downtown San Francisco traffic. I did not do this out of a strange compulsion to tempt fate but because the day prior I had signed up for the California AIDSRide, a 575-mile, week-long sojourn from San Francisco to Los Angeles to raise money for AIDS treatment and awareness. When I first heard about the event, I had trepidation: "Why not just drive your car? There is no way I'm going to ride my bike more than 500 miles in one week!"

However, I was drawn to the event not only by the desire to challenge myself but to serve a worthy cause. It is these guiding principles, to always push myself and to impact people beyond my own circle, that I look to for direction in all the things I do and something that I feel journalism fulfills. That is why I have chosen to pursue it as a profession, because to be able to write news that is relevant to people's lives is a way to tangibly serve society.

My primary job is as a reporter at *The Daily Deal*, a financial newspaper aimed at investment bankers, corporate lawyers and company executives. Knowing nothing of the complexities of the financial world, I was thrown into the job initially as an editorial assistant, which required me to write authoritatively for a very sophisticated audience. After about three months of intensive learning, I moved up from my post as an editorial assistant to reporter. It was and still is a daunting task, especially with the daily four-hour deadline, but I love the challenge.

My work as a freelance reporter at The Independent Newspaper Group, on the other hand, provides a whole new set of challenges and resplendent rewards. For The Independent I cover stories with a human aspect, issues that are relevant to the people of the local community. Whether I am covering the community service of a local congregation or the phenomenon of the ever-popular scooter, I enjoy the work because I can engage with people in the community and talk about issues important to them.

Working for two drastically different publications, I have learned that so much is determined by larger economic and political factors, but that it all ulti-mately trickles down to people on the local level. Making that connection with the community is incred-ibly rewarding, and to be able to extend my reach to a wider audience but retain the local interest is what I am ultimately aiming to do. A year abroad would provide the crucial stepping-stone toward that end.

Of course, the issues affecting local communities are most tangible when you experience them first hand through interactions with its less fortunate, some-thing I have always sought.

In Costa Rica, I found myself at the other end of this teacher-student spectrum. The seven months I spent living and studying at The University of Costa Rica were my first experience as a foreigner in a foreign land. Staying with a local family and attending univer-sity classes, I had no choice but to learn Spanish, and fast, at a level that six years of classroom instruction did not afford. In addition, I was in the middle of a crash course in Central American culture and the pertinent issues to the people there, and it was that experience of fully delving into Costa Rican life that imbued me with a passion for the region.

I took that passion to Washington D.C. where I worked as an intern for The Center for Strategic and International Studies, a foreign policy think tank. While there, I worked for The Mexico Project, a program that brought together dignitaries from both sides of the border to foster a unified binational policy. My time in Guatemala also is what fueled my desire to work closely with the Americas Program director to coauthor an election study of that country's presidential race that was disseminated throughout Capitol Hill. Writing that piece for a crowd so far removed from the issues highlighted what I have found to be a recurring dichotomy between the local concerns of one community and the disconnect with a potential audience so many miles away. That is the gap I want to be able to bridge.

It has been three years since I used Spanish in my daily life in Costa Rica, and I desperately want to reach the level of fluency necessary to use in a public forum. In seeking to go abroad once more I intend to do so, as well as get the formal journalistic education to buttress my practical training. Moreover, I could absorb the sense of a foreign society, history and culture that is only attainable through living the daily experience of another country. I would then be equipped to communicate more effectively and to a much wider audience, taking into account the sensibilities of another people and culture and balancing that with the knowledge I have from my own.

Cecilia A. Oleck, Knight Ridder Minority Scholar

Cecilia has competed athletically on the court, field and track. But it's her sense of competition in the newsroom that makes her want to pursue a career in journalism. While a student at West Catholic High School in Grand Rapids, Michigan, she wrote for the newspaper, tackling topics such as the double standards for athletes and gender stereotypes. As a result of her journalism experience, she won over $80,000 in awards including the Knight Ridder Minority Journalism Scholarship and a scholarship from the *Detroit Free Press*, where she has worked as an intern. A student at Saint Mary's College in South Bend, Indiana, she is majoring in communications, preparing for a career in journalism.

The Right Fit

For more people, the future is uncertain; the direction their life will take is not spelled out for them. Each person is responsible for the choices she will make that will determine the course of her life. One of the choices that has an incredible impact on her life is what she will choose for her career.

This can be a difficult decision to make, as it will affect almost every aspect of a person's life to some degree. Most people are also not fortunate enough to receive a startling revelation directing them on the right course for their lives. Instead, the most powerful way that a person is able to determine her direction is not through an earthshaking revelation but through the quiet confidence that this is what she is called to do and to be.

In the same way, I have never received any startling revelations that I should pursue a career in journalism, but as I look back on my life, I am able to see that there were many little steps along the way that have led me to this choice. I have often heard my parents tell the story of how, on my first day of kindergarten, I came home crying because I had not been taught how to read. I have always loved to read and from that has developed a great respect and fascination for the written word.

Joseph Pulitzer stated the purpose of a journalist should be to "Put it before them briefly so they will read it, clearly so they will appreciate it, picturesquely so they will remember it, and above all, accurately so they will be guided by its light." His words serve as a reminder for me of the many different dimensions of writing. Journalism encompasses both creativity and technicality. It is a way of expressing individuality and of communicating with others.

Many of my personal qualities convince me that a career in journalism is my calling. I find that I am a person who responds well to challenges. Perhaps it is because of my competitive nature that challenges motivate me, and I discover that my biggest competitor is usually myself. I think this is why I enjoy trying to combine both the creative and technical aspects of writing. Each time I begin to write, I am presented with a fresh challenge.

Every day that I live, I realize more the impact other people have on me and the impact I have on them. Writing is a very personal way of reaching out to people I may never meet, but who I am still connected to because of our identities as human beings. Journalism allows the opportunity for the sharing of information, thoughts, feelings and ideas between people from all walks of lives. It enables people to see things through another's eyes and gain new perspectives on the world around them.

It is because of the many dimensions of journalism that I desire to pursue a career in this field. I feel that as a journalist, I will be able to use the talents that I already have, as well as learn new ones. I believe it is a chance for me to be an instrument to bring people together.

Chris Kennedy, National Merit Semi-Finalist

From Leawood, Kansas, Chris has always been around animals. He has volunteered at a wildlife rehabilitation center, studied butterflies and moths and worked for his family's canine rescue group. In the ninth grade, Chris and his parents decided that he should be home-schooled so he could better pursue his interests. In addition to studying at home, he has remained active in local science groups and taken courses from a charter high school and college. With this essay on his plans to become an avian veterinarian, he was recognized as a National Merit Semi-Finalist. He gives this advice on applying for scholarships: "Don't put it off. The closer it gets to the deadline, the more terrifying it becomes. So start now."

Avian Veterinarian

I am the only person I know who dreams of becoming an avian veterinarian. That's a bird doctor if your Latin is rusty. I got my first bird--a cockatiel named Sunny for his cheerful disposition--slightly over a year ago. One look into those sweet, intelligent eyes, and I was hooked.

I first gained experience caring for birds of prey, songbirds and waterfowl volunteering with Operation Wildlife, a wildlife rehabilitation and education center that serves the eastern half of Kansas. One particularly memorable day at the center had me tube-feeding a hummingbird. I also participate in the Idalia Society, a group of lepidopterists that studies butterflies, moths and their environments. The magic of nature has always fascinated me, and I am lucky to have found a passion that will let me explore the world of birds and nature in my eventual career.

After seventh grade I chose unorthodox schooling that allowed me to explore my avian interests in more depth while still covering all academic subjects at an advanced level. I have thus pursued a blend of home-school, public school and college coursework. Each year's educational program has been different. In ninth grade I chose a year of home-schooling in literature and world history comple-mented with work at the college level in geology and biology at Johnson County Community College and volun-teering with Operation Wildlife and Farley's Angels, my family's private canine-rescue effort.

At the end of that year I decided I wanted to earn a Kansas Regent's high school diploma but also wanted to continue working at my own pace, exploring topics with greater depth than might be possible in a high school classroom. Those goals came together at Basehor-Linwood Virtual Charter School. I am completing the four-year curriculum in three years, substituting college courses in the sciences. Thanks to the Basehor-Linwood program I have had the latitude to pursue my interest in one facet of my heritage by substituting three years of intensive immersion education in Norwegian for more traditional language programming. At home, I'm currently completing Cornell Ornithology Lab's Bird Biology distance learning course, the University of Missouri-Columbia honors physics course and continuing my volunteer work.

My hard work earned me prizes in physics in the Kansas City Science Fair, in science and social studies in the State of Kansas Scholarship Contest and recognition at the national level by Duke University's Talent Identification (TIP) Program. My unusual curriculum allowed me to compete with students from traditional academic backgrounds while serving my interests as no public school could.

Boy Scouts gave me the chance to enjoy the outdoors while learning about myself and others and gaining valuable leadership skills. I applied those leadership lessons last summer in the American Legion Boys' State of Kansas, a once-in-a-lifetime opportunity to learn about state government. Together these programs taught me about the importance of individual participation and good leadership in groups.

At the most basic level my goals are like those of many others. I want to find the best college environment, study my chosen field of biology or pre-veterinary medicine, go to graduate school and have a fulfilling career. Of course, my particular career goal—to start my own avian veterinary clinic—is unusual, but it serves the same human need. I hope to be a good husband and father, to learn from mistakes, help others and do the right thing while remaining young at heart. With my preparation thus far and a lot more hard work, I will achieve my goals.

Andrea Setters, Dow Scholarship Winner

While she had always known that her future was in the sciences, it took an inspiring teacher for Andrea to discover that her passion was for chemistry. Her teacher at Fairborn High School in Fairborn, Ohio, taught her about the laws of thermodynamics, periodic trends, redox reactions and moles, and in doing so also became a mentor and friend. Andrea says about her teacher, "She brought out the best in me."

Andrea, majoring in chemistry, won scholarships including the Dow Chemistry Scholarship and Furman Founder's Scholarship to attend Furman University in South Carolina. She hopes to eventually earn a Ph.D. and work in pharmaceutical research.

Scientific Inspiration

I often sit in front of blank pieces of notebook paper and half-finished applications wondering why in the world I am still doing all this, wishing it were all over a little sooner. After all, basket weavers make a nice living: they create wonderful pieces with both aesthetic and functional purposes and I bet they didn't have to fill out 20-page questionnaires about what they have done with every waking hour of their lives for the last four years. Then again, I don't have any desire to be a basket weaver. Honestly, I would not have the slightest clue how to begin a basket and I hate splinters. I do, however, have a love of chemistry and it is this love that pushes me to continue with all the forms and essays with a little more enthusiasm than I may have started them with.

When I began to consider future careers, I set two basic criteria: I had to be decent at it, and it had to be something I never seemed to grow tired of. Science became the obvious answer. The not-so-easy question became what I wanted to do with science and what specific discipline. Then, during my sophomore and junior years, two experiences helped narrow down my field: my chemistry classes and being a teaching aide.

When I signed up for honors chemistry, I had absolutely no idea what I was getting myself into. I soon discovered, however, that I had nothing to worry about. The guidance gods smiled on me when they were assigning classes and I was placed in Mrs. Roshto's class. Mrs. Roshto's teaching ability and knowledge of chemistry continue to amaze me to this day. She had the knack to get to know each of her students personally and then be able to offer individual direction. I progressed through the class in a constant state of awe with the new world that was being opened to my eyes each day. I knew chemistry was the field I wanted to devote the rest of my life to.

My junior year I took AP Chemistry, which was also taught by Mrs. Roshto, and during my study hall I aided her Chemistry I class. The positive influence Mrs. Roshto had over so many students was inspiring and I fell in love with the idea that I could introduce students to this world of chemistry that they never could have imagined before. It was during that year that I decided teaching would become one of my career aspirations.

I have solved part of my original dilemma by finding that chemistry is the scientific field I want to work with most. I have yet to discover that perfect career but I believe with classroom experience and guidance I can find it and be able to devote myself to it wholeheartedly.

Essays About Leadership

Swati Deshmukh, Discover Card Tribute Award Scholarship Winner

Swati has helped collect 500 pairs of shoes for hurricane victims in India, raised funds for flood victims in Venezuela and spearheaded a bottled water sale fundraiser to aid flood victims in Mozambique. And these are just some of her efforts abroad.

At home at East Lyme High School in Connecticut, Swati has committed herself to public service, crocheting blankets for premature babies, tutoring students who are refugees from Burma and organizing a book drive for needy libraries.

It is her service and leadership that helped her become one of the nine national winners of the Discover Card Tribute Award. In addition to volunteering, Swati has won numerous awards for her writing, including first place in her state for the National History Day competition. Academically, she has a passion for research, studying organic synthesis of piezoelectric molecules as a participant in NASA's Sharp Program. She would like to eventually attend medical school.

A Fight Against Discrimination

One good example of my continuing leadership is my efforts to diminish prejudice and spread feelings of well-being throughout the school. Nearly all of the students who attend my school are white, and I am in a very small minority. For this reason, I feel almost obliged or rather chosen to carry the torch and lead the warriors of unbiased acceptance in an endless war against discrimination.

At the end of my freshman year, I wrote a proposal for a Multi-Cultural Club to recognize and celebrate the minorities at our school. However, the school felt that this subject was covered by other clubs. Disagreeing with the administration, a faculty member at my school invited me to visit Westbrook High School where the Anti-Defamation League was running its program "Names Can Really Hurt Us."

Amazed at what I saw, I labored to bring this program to my school to combat our problems. I convinced my principal to let the Anti-Defamation League come to our school, and I raised the $4,500 that was necessary. With faculty members and other students, I formed the Diversity Team to help run the program. We selected 30 students to form the team, which would be trained by the ADL to help lead the program.

Now, every other week, I run meetings for the Diversity Team in which we prepare for the program. I have set up an e-mail system to contact them, and I have organized a special retreat for us. I also initiated a paper chain project in which every student in the school was given a slip of paper to decorate. The slips of paper will be linked together to form a chain.

My efforts to combat prejudice in the school have turned me into a leader of my peers. In guiding and directing others, I have discovered that I have the ability to lead others and motivate them to achieve great things. I plan to continue my leadership and maintain diversity programs at our school.

Academic Accomplishments

Jonathan Bloom, National Merit Scholarship Winner

When applying for the National Merit Scholarship, Jonathan chose to write about the subject for which he has the most passion—mathematics. While still a student at West Bloomfield High School in Michigan, he took college level math courses and conducted research through an internship with General Motors. He advises other students applying for awards to write about their interests. He says, "They have many students to choose from so you can't be too modest or you won't stand out. Be excited, tell them your passions and write with a goal in mind." Jonathan is studying mathematics at Harvard University and plans to pursue a career in the field. In addition to math, he enjoys tae kwon do, volunteering at a student-run homeless shelter and juggling knives, torches and balls.

Cryptography & Encryption

I would like to pursue an academic life in the field of mathematics. This interest in mathematics developed not only through my coursework but more importantly through my independent research. After successfully completing AP Calculus BC and AP Physics as a sophomore, I felt the need for a greater challenge than that derived from "spoon-fed" instruction. Therefore, the following summer, I attended the Ross Young Scholars Program at Ohio State University. While fully immersed in number theory for eight weeks, I developed a burning hunger for the in-depth study of mathematics. I learned how to think scientifically and perform research independently. The founder of the program honored me with an invitation to return as a junior counselor.

During my junior year, I used a graduate text to guide my research in one of the most active fields of applied number theory, cryptography. My investigation into both public and private key cryptosystems led to an award-winning science project through the development of software, which demonstrated RSA and other encryption algorithms. I completed my directed study in the area of cryptography for 500-level credit at Wayne State University.

Last summer, instead of returning to Ohio State, I completed an internship in the Operations Research Department of the General Motors Truck Group. I conducted a study that identified the most efficient method for accurately approximating the vehicle weight distribution for their product lines. Ten weeks later, I had completed the project, documented the results and given five presentations to increasing levels of management. General Motors is now looking at ways to quickly implement my findings, which will result in the company saving millions of dollars. The vice president has requested that I return next summer.

Currently, in addition to taking 400- and 500-level math courses, I am conducting an independent study at the University of Michigan-Dearborn. I am constructing the first small-scale prototype of "The Weizmann Institute Key Locating Engine" (TWINKLE). As described by Adi Shamir in 1998, this device utilizes optoelectronics to factor large integers presently considered not factorable, effectively threatening the security of 512-bit RSA encryption. The project requires extensive knowledge in mathematics, computer science and electrical engineering. My research has the full support of my faculty advisor, a Ph.D. in mathematics and professor in the CIS department. Professors at three universities have expressed an interest in my progress. Even if I don't reach my goal of a working model for the science fair this spring, I will still have amassed a tremendous amount of knowledge.

As chairman of our school's Science Research Committee and president of the National Honor Society, I have the opportunity to personally encourage classmates to do independent research and to facilitate their entry into the Science and Engineering Fair of Metropolitan Detroit. I hope that I am able to instill into some of my classmates even a fraction of the enthusiasm and motivation that I gained from the Ross Young Scholars Program. With the desire in place, the opportunities are endless.

Note: Jonathan makes one clarification about his essay. He was able to construct only part of the TWINKLE device. However he says, it wasn't "such a disappointment. It's just that my original goal was a little too ambitious."

Svati Singla, Discover Card Tribute Award Scholarship Winner

11-Year-Old Scientist

As an active and innovative student, I am always seeking unique opportunities that will broaden my realm of experience. At a very early age, I became involved in the field of scientific research as a very unique endeavor.

Though I was only 11 years old, I was determined not to let my age hinder my extreme ambition and interest in higher level research. Thus, I independently contacted the head of the Nuclear Cardiology Department at the local university and requested the opportunity to conduct research in his laboratory. Recognizing my genuine interest and scientific aptitude, he immediately introduced me to the lab methods and I began a detailed study, which demanded many hours of my time.

Since I was extremely young, I found the research concepts to be very difficult in the beginning; however, with determination and a positive mental outlook, I was able to comprehend all the research methods. The findings of my research were very significant and were published in the *American Journal of Hypertension*.

After the conclusion of this study, I continued my interest in research by initiating another experimental study in the Department of Biochemistry. This study dealt with drug abuse during pregnancy and fetal alcohol syndrome. The research was presented at local science competitions and was awarded top honors by the U.S. Army and Navy.

Another challenging activity, which I initiated, was to coach a young Odyssey of the Mind team. Odyssey of the Mind is a program that encourages creative thinking, problem solving, and teamwork; I have been involved in this program for over six years and have found it to be a rewarding experience. Thus, when a group of interested first and second graders needed a coach for their team, I readily stepped up and volunteered to accept this massive responsibility. It is very rare for students to coach Odyssey of the Mind teams. Thus, this was a very creative and unique endeavor, which I initiated for the benefit of the young team. Though it was a strenuous time commitment, I obtained a priceless feeling of satisfaction knowing that this had been a positive experience for everyone who was involved.

Both of these unique endeavors have taught me that age should never be a hindrance in the way of learning or sharing knowledge with others.

Emily Heikamp, Angier B. Duke Memorial Scholarship Winner

When exploring colleges in high school, it took Emily and her mother 14 hours to drive from Metairie, Louisiana, to the North Carolina campus of Duke University. But it was time well spent. After her visit, Emily fell in love with the college. She later wrote this essay to gain admission to and earn a full-tuition scholarship from Duke. In all, the self-described "science nerd" earned over $250,000 in scholarships including full-tuition awards from Texas A&M and Tulane University, which she declined to attend her dream school. A graduate of Archbishop Chapelle High School, she is majoring in biology and mathematics and plans to earn an M.D.Ph.D. in immunology or oncology.

Science Nerd

AGTCCGGAATT is the genetic code for Tumor Necrosis Factor (TNF), a human cytokine that may have deleterious, even fatal effects if produced in excess or inadequate quantities. For the past two years, I have performed research to study the effects of alcohol and glucocorticoids on the TNF response in murine macrophage cells. One may ask why I am interested in such an obscure topic. Well, I am a science nerd.

Scientific research fascinates me, as experiments raise many questions and always provide new challenges. Research also supplies knowledge of the most intimate interactions of the human body, giving a glimpse of processes that are invisible to the naked eye. My research provides me with this knowledge and the ability to share it with others, and it has given my life direction and purpose.

I discovered my passion for research when I was 15 years old. The summer after my sophomore year, I decided to trade in cherished lazy afternoons with tennis buddies, waking up at 1 p.m. and two months of dormancy for my tired brain. I became an employee of the physiology department at Louisiana State University Medical Center. My buddies became lab technicians, I woke up at 7 a.m. instead of sleeping in and my tired brain was forced into overdrive as I learned about Tumor Necrosis Factor and Lipopolysaccharides. And I loved my job.

I worked for Dr. Gregory Bagby, a professor and researcher of the Alcohol Research Center at LSUMC. His lab studies the effects of Simian Immunodeficiency Virus and Ethanol on Rhesus Macaques. In other words, how SIV-infected drunken monkeys can get really sick. Nonetheless, his research fascinated me, and I had so many questions. Perhaps what fascinated me even more was Dr. Bagby spent time explaining his world of Lipopolysaccharides (LPS) and Tumor Necrosis Factor (TNF) to me, a lowly high school sophomore! I began to perform experiments and assays for his lab, while also doing secretarial work for his research grants. Eventually, I began my own research on alcohol and stress hormones. My research taught me so much and gave my life new direction. I finally knew what career I would pursue. But more importantly, I learned what kind of researcher I want to be. Dr. Bagby had shown me that being a great scientist is more than Nobels, prestige, and grant money. It is about sharing what you have learned with others, even lowly high school sophomores!

Being able to work with others who share my passion and enthusiasm has helped me to shape my dream. I plan to earn an M.D.Ph.D., specializing in immunology. As a physician scientist, I will see patients while also performing research to find new medications or a cure for their illnesses. I feel blessed to be a healthy young

woman, and so I want to serve those who are not as fortunate by doing what I love most--research.

More Essay Advice From The Winners
Scholarship Winners

Here are some more tips on crafting your essay from scholarship winners.—Gen & Kelly

Jason Morimoto
U.C. Berkeley student and scholarship winner
"The way to shine is by crafting a story in your essay that brings out your strengths. I like to give a lot of personal examples as to why I am involved in certain activities. I try to avoid the generic responses like 'it was a good learning experience' or 'I wanted to try something new.' For example, I often use the example of how I walked on to a national champion rugby team as a mere 5'6" player with no prior experience. The coach took one look at me and wanted to laugh. I told him that all I wanted was a tryout. With a lot of determination and hard work, I proved myself capable of playing with world class athletes."

Kristin N. Javaras
Rhodes Scholar
"I highly recommend showing it to people who have won fellowships themselves or who have read successful fellowship application essays before (and the more people the better). Also, I feel that the revision process was crucial for my essay: I went through about seven or eight drafts of my personal statement!"

Essays About Athletics

Sara Bei, CIF Scholar-Athlete Of The Year

From Montgomery High School in Santa Rosa, California, Sara was still excited about her team's underdog victory at the state cross country meet when she wrote this essay. One of the most profound lessons that she learned was how to motivate her team, a topic she uses as the centerpiece of this essay. Along with a half-tuition scholarship to Stanford, Sara also won over $6,000 in scholarships. She encourages all students to be relentless about applying for scholarships since in her words, "sometimes the ones you end up winning are the one you almost didn't apply to."

Inspiring Greatness

As a three-time state cross country champion entering my senior year, I hadn't expected this season to be much different than the others. I planned on working hard to achieve my goal of winning state, and I looked forward to having fun with my teammates in the process. In previous years, our girls team hadn't been very motivated, leaving me to take it upon myself to make it to state as an individual. Little did I know that a completely different challenge lay ahead of me for my senior year.

At the beginning of the year, I was pleasantly surprised to find two newcomers fresh out of junior high, who had decided to come out for the team to give us the fourth and fifth runners that we so desperately needed. Immediately I began to ponder what our team's potential was, and as always, I shot high. I organized a team sleep-over and, while beading necklaces and watching movies, tried to instill in them the goal of winning the state championship. Most of them were doubtful, even shocked, that I thought a team who failed to even make it to the state meet the previous year could have a shot at winning it. However, I was prepared to help them to not only realize their potential and believe in themselves, but to work together as a group and strengthen one another in the process.

Throughout the road to the state meet, I was busy trying to find ways to motivate the girls to train harder. I gave them little weekly gifts and notes, made breakfast as incentive for morning runs before school, organized team bonding activities outside of practice and even made a "State Champion Challenge Chart." I tried everything possible to get them to do the necessary preparation to be the best, as well as have fun and come together as a team. In the process, I found myself devoting so much time to the team that I was hardly channeling any energy into my own training. Although this concerned my coach, I reassured her that by working with the team, we were helping each other and improving together.

Finally, the day arrived in a flutter of nerves, anxiety and excitement. After giving them a pep talk, we toed the line together and I thought back on all the months we spent training, planning and dreaming for this moment. True, I was out to become the first person to win four state titles, but as I chanted our cheer with each of the girls, I realized that my real drive to win was coming from our team's need for every point we could get. That day, we upset the first- and second-ranked teams, with each girl running the race of her lifetime to become the Division II State Champions! Seeing the smiles and tears of pure joy on the faces of my teammates, I realized that beyond the medals and championships, there lies a treasure of value that far surpasses any other individual award in inspiring greatness in others.

Artistic Talents

Andrew Koehler, Fulbright Grant Winner

Andrew has been a serious student of music since he was 5 years old, when he first began to play the violin. Originally from Oreland, Pennsylvania, he has performed as a violinist with the Philadelphia Youth Orchestra, the Yale Symphony Orchestra and numerous festival orchestras. While at Yale, from which he graduated with honors as a double German Studies and Music major, he began to conduct seriously and is now pursuing a career in conducting. After spending a summer as a conducting student at the Aspen Music Festival and School, he is continuing his studies at the University for Music and Art in Vienna on a Fulbright Grant.

Turningpoint

My parents both spent the first part of their childhood overseas. As Ukrainian immigrants in America, they faced both the immediate difficulty of learning a new language and the eventual difficulty of acting as translators for their families, who never were able to learn English adequately. Though I, too, was raised speaking Ukrainian, my parents ultimately wanted to give me a means of communication that would transcend all others, a language of international recognition; this, they decided, was to be music.

The choice they gave me, for whatever reason, consisted of only two instruments: violin and piano. Such was the decision I was to make at the age of 5, when I might otherwise have been happier to continue playing uninterruptedly with my action figures. I arbitrarily chose violin, blissfully unaware of the impending consequences. I cannot pretend that something in my soul stirred the first time I held the instrument. I played dutifully enough, though I, like any other child, did not really enjoy practicing. I went through a long series of mediocre teachers who failed to generate any real excitement in me. They gave me enough encouragement, however, to realize that I had at least some talent, and with this ray of hope, my parents continued to push me.

Much later, during the first rehearsal of a youth orchestra I had recently joined, something astonishing oc-
curred. Sitting in the back of the section, I was intimidated in part by the music on the stand in front of me
but mostly by the conductor on the podium, an extraordi-
narily temperamental man who could be blisteringly honest
in passing judgment on one's abilities as a musician. We
began the rehearsal by sight-reading the first piece in
our program. We muddled through admirably enough, but he
was clearly unsatisfied. He leapt from his stool and
spat, "You play like you're older than I am," with each
strong syllable of his phrase strengthened by ferocious
baton swats on his stand. He paused and composed himself.
"Do you know what this music is about?" No one dared
breathe a word. He then spoke of love and death and of
the profound tragedy that links the two with an eloquence
unbefitting his audience. He stopped suddenly and dis-
gustedly offered, "but you don't understand; you're too
young," and then looked up at us questioningly, as if to
ask whether or not he was right. He might well have been,
but we desperately wanted to understand for that man. And
so we played again, and this time, I began to hear music
in an utterly different way, as did many, I suspect. His
passion for this art was simply infectious. Where I had
never previously known music to be more than just pleasant, I began to understand what defined greatness, both
in interpretation and in composition. Poor performances
could make me cringe, but the most sublime moments in
great performances made my hair stand on end. I began to
approach music with a penetrating enthusiasm which, save
for the charisma of a great teacher, might never have
been.

Years later, and as my focus shifts from violin to conducting, this enthusiasm continues only to strengthen.
Knowing the difficulties of a life in music, I have tried
seriously to pursue other interests, but no matter how
engaging I find them, none generate the same passion in
me that music does. I am resigned to my fate; I wish to
be a musician. It is a perilous fate that neither my
parents nor certainly I could have imagined when this
endeavor began, but it is a fate nevertheless tinged with
joy, for I may count myself among the few who have found
something they sincerely love.

Eddie Hollenbeck III, Imation Computer Arts Scholarship Winner

Eddie was a 15-year-old student at Oviedo High School in Florida when he started his own web design and hosting business. As a college student at the School of the Art Institute of Chicago, he juggles his classes with business meetings and several design positions at companies spanning the country. In addition to winning the Imation award, Eddie was selected as the Student Journalist of the Year by the Florida Scholastic Press Association and has won the *Orlando Sentinel* Rave Scholarship. His design work contributed to his high school newspaper being nationally recognized by the National Scholastic Press Association, and he served as the lead graphic designer for Rave, named the #1 Youth Section in the Nation by the Newspaper Association of America. Majoring in visual communication, film and multimedia, Eddie has also founded his own company, EH Independent Design. Below is Eddie's winning submission. The original color version can be seen on the Imation website at www.imation.com.

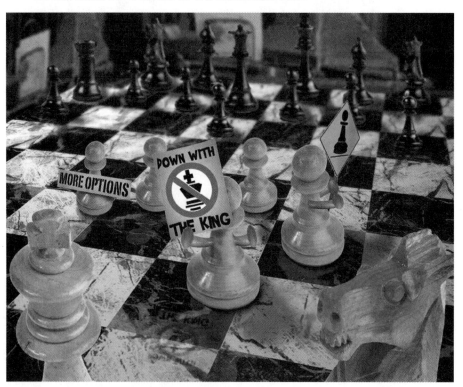

A Parent's Essay

Maggy Michaels, SuperCollege.com Parent Winner

Not all scholarships are for you—the student. There are a few that Mom and Dad can enter. One is sponsored by SuperCollege.com, which is also the publisher of this book. Since Mom and Dad are constantly hounding you to apply for scholarships, you can now give it right back to them and say, "Sure! But you have to also!"

This year's winner, Margaret, recalls that when she was in high school her father refused to pay for room and board. "I had no idea financial aid even existed, so I sacked my university dreams and attended a community college in my hometown," she says. Now that her daughter is heading off to college, Margaret is determined to give her the option of attending any school she desires. It was without question that she should apply to this scholarship when her daughter handed her the application and said, "You have to do this. Humor is part of the criteria, and if anyone can squeeze some laughs out of this whole thing, it's you."

Getting Katie Into College

Launching a kid into college is second only to labor and delivery for intensity of effort and ultimate reward--grunts and screams notwithstanding. Without a doubt, financing college is a daunting prospect for double-income families. As a single mom, my search for financial assistance had all the frantic focus of someone looking for a ground-level window in a burning building. Fortunately, hurdle Number One was an easy jump. Katie landed tuition waivers from all three state universities, which is particularly amazing when you consider how dramatically my genes watered down her father's IQ. The wild side of DNA can be a wondrous thing.

Katie's choice was the University of Arizona, located about 90 miles south of our front door. One glance at the price of a dorm room made me realize that hurdle Number Two would be a real challenge. Tuition waivers are nothing more than enticements to reserve a space the size of a shoebox in a building so pricey that it should be renamed The Trump Towers. Wouldn't you know, Katie turned up her nose at the idea of pitching a tent in a nearby park. She was actually indignant, as if I was suggesting that option for all four years. Kids are so spoiled these days.

The dynamic combination of my daughter's initiative fueled by my own seasoned nagging turned up glimmers of hope. We stumbled across excellent resources like the book *Get Free Cash for College* and tips from the Internet. The university financial aid department and Katie's high school counselor tossed us a few crumbs of information. Friends and relatives forwarded odd scholarship applications including one from Tylenol. As poetic as that seemed, something sponsored by Prozac or Valium might have been even more appropriate from my viewpoint.

The true depth of my financial anxiety surfaced as Katie and I pored over an application for a scholarship offered by my health insurance company. Geared toward young adults with an entrepreneurial spirit, the application called for a five-year business plan in addition to the grind of essays, transcripts, activities and letters of recommendation. Katie asked me to look over the fiscal data on her business plan, including estimates of capital outlay. When I grabbed my throat and asked for a paper bag to breathe into, my daughter rolled back her eyes and announced flatly, "You really need therapy, Mom."

She was absolutely right. Unfortunately, Mom's therapy will be hurdle Number Six. We still have Three, Four and Five to master before Katie is en route to capturing her sheepskin. One baby step at a time, we make our way. Instead of sighing with relief at the prospect of having enough money to cover one semester's dorm expense, the mantra that floats through my mind sounds more like, "Just 24 months, and I'll be going through this again with Elizabeth."

Seeking Genuineness
Coca-Cola Scholars Foundation

You may think that with the right mix of perseverance and success you can create a winning essay. The truth is that there is no single winning formula for creating a masterpiece. As you'll see in comments from the Coca-Cola Scholars Foundation, the best thing that you can do in your essay is be yourself. —Gen and Kelly

Beyond the essay topic provided, students participating at the Semifinalist level are given no instruction as to how to write their essays for the Coca-Cola Scholars Foundation's four-year Scholars Program.

"We don't provide instruction because we see the essay as an opportunity for each student to sincerely express themselves," says Trisha Bazemore, program assistant.

The 27 members of the Program Review Committee, comprised of college admission officers and high school guidance counselors, are chosen for their expertise in evaluating students' writing.

So what is the committee seeking as it reviews the 2,000 Semifinalist applications? In a word, genuineness.

"You can tell when you read an essay if it's 'real,' expressing an individual's heartfelt experience, or if it's an essay derived more from an awareness of presentation," says Bazemore. She says that it's important that students not try to write what they think the review committee wants to read.

"Be yourself," she says.

CHAPTER SIX

12 ESSAYS THAT BOMBED

In this chapter:

■ **12 disastrous essays**

■ **"Where's the Point"**

■ **"Attempted Tearjerker"**

■ **"Miss America"**

■ **"Behold! My Statistics"**

■ **"My Life as Seen on TV"**

Learning From Failure

History has shown that some of our greatest successes have been inspired by failure. Akio Morita's automatic rice cooker was a huge failure and burned the rice it was supposed to boil. In desperation, Morita and a partner turned to building cheap tape recorders. From this single product came Sony Corp. Across the ocean a high school coach cut a young varsity football player. That athlete's name was none other than Michael Jordan. The founder of the automobile industry, Henry Ford twice filed for bankruptcy before he finally stumbled onto the product that would launch his company, the Model T.

In keeping with history's tradition we bring you 12 essays that failed. These essays, however, provide an extremely important lesson: they help you learn what not to do. As you read each essay along with our comments you will understand why they fell short of the mark. While you are writing your essays, keep the lessons from this chapter in mind. These essay writers lost, but at least in doing so they are helping you to avoid the same fate.

Where's The Point?

Reading an essay without a point is like getting on an airplane without knowing where it's going. Yet many students turn in essays without any clear message. Consider the following essay and see if you can locate the message the author is trying to convey:

Where Has Time Gone?

As I sit at the lunch table, it suddenly hits me. Where has all the time gone? I am a senior in high school who is about to graduate in a matter of months and I have just realized that I might never see my friends after we receive our diplomas.

Surely we'll see each other at reunions, but what will become of the great moments that we have shared?

I will never forget when one of my friends and I were given the responsibility of putting together a class beach party. My friend wasn't a very creative or outgoing person, however, he was nearly twice as strong as me. So we came up with a plan. I would do all of the promotion for the party as well as decide the theme and menu. He would be responsible for making sure all of the food, sound equipment and decorations were transported to the beach. It was the perfect plan. Most of our classmates told us afterward that it was the best activity that they'd ever been to.

I sometimes wish I could stay in my school forever. I have learned so much in the last four years. Before I came to high school I didn't even know what I was capable of intellectually. My teachers have been some of the most inspirational people in my life.

I know that college will bring with it many new memories and experiences and I am looking forward to it. However, I will never forget the friends who stayed by my side and the teachers who cared throughout the good times and the bad.

Why This Essay Bombed

In this essay, the author simply has no meaning in his writing. The essay covers a range of feelings and experiences. By the end of the essay we wonder what we just read. Is the point that the author will miss his friends? Is it that he is able to solve the problem of working with a friend who is not creative or outgoing? Or is it that his teachers have been the most influential people in his life? There is no connection between the disjointed ideas. We are left confused and unimpressed.

How To Avoid This Mistake

As you are writing, think about what you are trying to convey. Ask the question, "What's the significance of this essay?" If you can't answer this question in a single sentence, then it probably means you need to make your message stronger and more clearly defined.

Since you often have limited space for your essay, it is better to stick to a single topic. Select one and develop it throughout your essay. Don't confuse the scholarship committee by writing about a number of things that have little or no connection to each other.

The Attempted Tearjerker

There were few dry eyes at the end of the movie "Titanic," and the director wanted it that way. Movies about tragedy are intended to evoke emotion from viewers. Some students do the same thing with their scholarship essay, attempting to win the reader over with dejected accounts of loss, desperation and hopelessness.

Unfortunately, these essays do not appeal to scholarship judges. They do not want to read about how difficult your past has been except within the context of how you've faced the challenges or your plans for improving your situation. They want to be inspired by what you have done and see that you are working to make your life better.

My So-Called Life

Someone once said, "Life is like a bowl of cherries-- sometimes it's the pits." There could be no more accurate saying to describe my life thus far.

Even before I was born there was trouble. When my mother was pregnant she got into a car accident and nearly lost her baby--me! While I don't recall this event it was clearly an omen of things to come.

Throughout my childhood my parents were never rich. I remember one Christmas how jealous I was when I went back to school and my friends had the newest clothes and toys. Sure, I got gifts but not the kind of expensive presents that my friends had received.

When I was 15 years old I returned home one day and noticed that something was different. Half of the stuff that we owned in our apartment was gone. We had

been robbed. The burglar had taken most of the good
stuff that we owned. That year my brothers and I had
to share a single 21-inch television.

As if things could not get any worse, the next year I
learned that I had diabetes. While not life threatening it was enough to send me into a depression that
took months to get out from.

Now that I am about to graduate I feel lucky to even
be here given the hardships of my past 17 years. Going
to college has been a life-long dream. This scholarship would help me pay for college and build a better
life.

Why This Essay Bombed

While it is hard to not feel sympathy for an applicant who has
suffered misfortunes and hardships, there are almost no scholarships that give money based on how much you have suffered.
Rather scholarship judges want to see how you have excelled
despite the obstacles in your life. The focus should be on what
you have accomplished or what you plan to accomplish in spite
of setbacks.

How To Avoid This Mistake

If your past has been a rough one, you can certainly write about
it. But don't expect the hardships themselves to make your essay
a winner. Make sure you include what you have achieved or what
you have learned from these challenges. Write about how the
hardships will influence you or affect your future. While scholarship judges know that many students have had to endure difficulties, what they want to see is someone who has survived and
thrived.

Miss America Essay

We've all seen the Miss America Pageants. And we've all heard
(and made fun of) the speeches contestants make. "I want to cure
the world of hunger," "I want to save and give back to mother

nature" and "I want to make sure that every person on the planet has a place they can happily call home." These ideals are just too lofty to take seriously. It is amazing how many scholarship applicants write about these very ideals that, despite their good intentions, are just too idealistic to be considered seriously.

My Dedication To The World

Through five years of community service, I've learned many things. I've seen the empty hearts in the children without parents and the broken hearts of seniors who get no visitors. Because of these experiences, I've learned that only through service I can be a fulfilled person.

Therefore, I have decided to work to end the suffering of all people who face the perils of being without food, clothing or shelter. This is now my life goal.

After college I plan to start a shelter for orphans. This orphanage will take care of children who have been abandoned and will attempt to create as normal a family life as possible. Once my first orphanage is established I will branch out to other areas and countries. My dream is to build a global network that would once and for all end the suffering of children.

Once I have accomplished this I plan on running for public office so that I can affect change on an even broader scale. As senator or president I will make laws and convince other countries to do what they can to protect each and every human. For it is only by committing ourselves to ending human suffering that progress can be made.

As humans we are here to make the world a better place, and if each person does his or her part, like I plan to do, the world *would* be a much better place.

Why This Essay Bombed

The applicant's heart is in the right place but the ideas are just too farfetched to be taken seriously. This just sounds too much like a Miss America answer and does not show that the applicant has any basis in reality.

How To Avoid This Mistake

This type of essay should be avoided altogether. There's no doubt that if each of us were given the chance, we would end world-wide hunger or save Mother Nature, but let's face it, this isn't realistic. Focusing on a few issues and describing what you have done can make a great essay. Keep your positive attitude and enthusiasm but ground your ideas in reality, and focus on what you have done instead of what you would do in a limitless world.

The Life-Changing Voyage

Whether backpacking across Europe or climbing Mt. McKinley, students travel the world and bring home countless memories and experiences. Travel, thus, is a common topic when it comes to essays. However, too often essays about travel make common sweeping generalizations, are merely depictions of the superficial aspects of the trip or try to cover the events of two weeks in two pages. Here is an example of a travel essay gone awry:

```
              My Trip To Europe

Two years ago I had the privilege of traveling to six
European countries. There I met many interesting
people and saw many interesting sights. In England I
got to stand next to the guard who cannot be disturbed
from his upright, staring position. In France I got to
look out to the horizon from the famous Eiffel Tower.
In Belgium I ate frites, which are essentially Belgian
french fries. In Germany I saw where the Berlin Wall
stood not too many years ago. In Italy I saw the
```

Colosseum, where the Gladiators fought. And finally, in Switzerland I saw the Alps and ate fondue.

Besides having a great time seeing new places and meeting new faces, I also learned a great deal about the cultures of different European countries. I learned that people from different countries are, well, different. They have different mindsets about certain aspects of life and different ways of thinking. However, I also learned that people are, in a way, all the same. All the different ideas and concepts centered on the same areas of thinking and are therefore merely different interpretations of the same thing.

My visit to Europe has definitely changed my view of the world. I hope that someday everyone will have a chance to visit Europe or another foreign land and learn how diverse and similar our world really is.

Why This Essay Bombed

This essay is too much of a diary of sights seen, activities done and food eaten. Virtually *any* student who visited Europe could have written this—and many will. The essay also makes a common general observation of travelers—while people from different countries have differences we are all essentially the same. The result is that this essay hardly stands out from any other essay about travel.

How To Avoid This Mistake

Whether your travels have taken you to the Museé du Louvre in Paris or your grandmother's house in Tulsa, you probably have numerous experiences that could become good essays. However, when you're considering your possibilities, try to separate those events that could happen to many travelers from those that were truly unique to your visit. Focus on a specific event and elaborate on what that has taught you or how it has affected your life. Instead of writing about all seven days of your travel, narrow it to one day or even one hour. Also avoid sweeping generalizations about the people of a country or humanity at large.

Convoluted Vocabulary

How many times have you read a passage in a standardized test or in an advanced work of literature and found that each word made you more confused than the last? If used properly, word choice can convey sophistication and demonstrate a writer's command of the language. However, when used incorrectly or only to impress, the results are convoluted, conceited or just plain incorrect. Here is an example of an essay that was intended to awe. See if you are impressed enough with this writer to hand over your money.

Educationality

That education is my utmost priorative focus is verified in my multitude of academic, extracurricular and intercurricular activities. I insinuate myself in learning and acquiring a plethora of knowledge. I am a person that doesn't approbate no for an answer when it comes to enhancing the prominence of my mind.

This pontifical accolade is an integral part of my scholarization, and without it, my temperament would fall short of instructured. My transcendent achievements speak for themselves and deserve accolades.

Why This Essay Bombed

It appears as if this essay had a head-on collision with a thesaurus. Using SAT words is fine as long as you use them correctly. Scholarship judges are not interested in how complicated a sentence you can construct, but rather how meaningful you can make it. Plus, some of the words this applicant uses were made up!

How To Avoid This Mistake

Don't venture into areas of the English language where you are a stranger. It is okay to use multisyllabic words when you see fit, but to use big words just for the sake of using them is a mistake.

Behold! My Statistics

Have you ever read the back of a baseball card? It is filled with statistics reflecting the player's performance during the season. It may show that a player is one of the fastest men on the field or that he performs well in the playoffs, but the statistics say nothing about a player as a person. Keep this in mind when writing your scholarship application essays. If you just list your statistics such as GPA, classes and activities, the judges will never get meaningful insight into who you really are.

My Name Is Brooke

Hello, my name is Brooke. I will be a senior at Central High School in Topeka, Kansas.

I was born on October 29. I have interests in writing and mathematics. My schedule junior year was as follows: AP English Language, Honors Physics, AP Calculus AB, AP United States History, Honors III Spanish and P.E. My extracurricular activities are varsity cheer and Key Club.

Here are my standardized test scores: 1370 SAT I, 620 SAT II Writing, 610 SAT II US History, 680 SAT II Math IIC, 4 on AP English, 3 on AP US history and 3 on AP Calculus.

I have worked hard throughout my four years in high school to maintain a 3.7 GPA. I plan to graduate with honors next year. From there I will go to college.

I plan to major in either communications or business in college. The reason I will major in either communications or business is because I love to work with people and I am seriously interested in getting into the entertainment industry.

My favorite subjects in school this past year were AP English and AP Calculus. My hobbies include sewing,

```
playing piano, singing and writing short stories. I
currently have a job at a local restaurant.
```

Why This Essay Bombed

This essay gives a lot of information about the writer but it says almost nothing about her motivation, dreams or beliefs. These are what scholarship judges want to know. They want a sense of who you are. This isn't conveyed through a list of your statistics. Also, the application often asks for most of this information. So why repeat your list of activities, classes and GPA when the scholarship judges already have your application and transcript?

How To Avoid This Mistake

It's easy to write an essay in which you rattle off your status in life and a list of your accomplishments. What's more difficult is putting your place in life and achievements into perspective and making sense of them. Focus on a few of your more important achievements and expand on those. Since the application form has a place to list your activities, grades and test scores, don't repeat them in the essay. Use the essay to go beyond your statistics and provide context for their significance.

The Most Influential Person In The World

A common essay topic is the person who has had the most influence on your life. You can imagine the countless essays that students write about parents, grandparents, siblings, friends and idols. The challenge is to write about this influential person in a way that is different from what other students write and that reveals something about you as well. This essay falls short on both counts.

```
                    I Love My Family

There is no one person who has had the most influence
in my life; instead, it is a group. That group con-
```

sists of the most important people in my life: my family. My family is made up of four people: my mom, my dad, my younger sister and me. My parents are my role models; they provide the home in which I live, the food that I eat and the money to buy essential items. They have set for me a good example of what kind of life I should lead. They have always been there for me, through the good times and the bad, to support, love and cherish me.

My mom, in particular, has always been very supportive of me. She has been the one to tell me bedtime stories when I go to sleep. She has been my unacknowledged chauffeur, taking me places such as the occasional baseball game or regular piano lesson even if she had more important things to do.

My father, on the other hand, has always been the advice giver. To me, he is all knowing, for he always has a good answer to the questions I have. My father, who is an engineer, helps me with my math and science homework; I wouldn't be as successful at math if it weren't for him. I love both my parents because they have both contributed to my life so much.

My sister has also played an important role in my life. She has always helped me whenever I was in need; when I couldn't solve a problem, when I couldn't think of a good design for my visual aid or just when I needed someone to talk to. I love my sister, and even though I'd be embarrassed to tell it to her face, she's my best friend. And even though we might fight every so often about issues we shouldn't even care about, our friendship is a strong one; those fights are just testaments to how real it really is.

Why This Essay Bombed

The problem with this essay is that it is too ordinary. Many applicants will write about what their parents do for them and how they hope to pattern their lives after them. This essay just does not stand out.

Be True
Elisa Juárez & Emanuel Pleitez

Being truthful in your essay is not just the right thing to do but it also makes for a much better essay. Many essay disasters are created when authors decide to write about something they don't know much or care about.—Gen & Kelly

Elisa Tatiana Juárez
Brown University student and scholarship winner
"Be honest. I have a lot of friends who said you could lie. You could but in the end people will really know who you are."

Emanuel Pleitez
Stanford University student and scholarship winner
"Be true. Don't try to fake anyone out. It's not going to work. You don't have to be the greatest writer. I write what I really feel. If you really believe in what you're writing, then you should be well off."

How To Avoid This Mistake

It may be difficult for you to choose just one person who stands above the rest. And the person you select may be mom or dad. These essays will work if, and *only* if, a unique angle is taken. A generic description about your father, such as, "My father is always there for me, through the good times and the bad," will get you nowhere. It's important to be as specific as possible in describing exactly what it is that you admire about your father. Fortunately, there are unique things about all of our siblings, parents, friends and idols that make them special. Focus on those aspects.

Creativity Overload

We've all heard the various analogies for life—"life is like a box of chocolates," "life is a sport" and so on. Wouldn't it be clever if, somehow, you could create your *own* analogy of life? Surely it would show how deep of a thinker you are and how well you can write, right? Being clever is usually good. But sometimes you can take it too far, wearing out a novel idea.

The Highway Of Life

Life is like a highway with cars going in all directions. People are constantly coming and going from all sorts of places. Sometimes, when too many people want to go to the same place, traffic jams form, just when too many people apply for a single position at a company.

The Highway Patrol is akin to my parents because whenever I feel like breaking the rules, as any driver would, the presence of my parents always prevents me from doing so.

Throughout my young life I have been on a highway full of cars passing interesting exits. As I pass each exit--the doctor exit, the lawyer exit, the CEO exit-- I realize that my highway of life is full of so many possibilities.

However, none of these intriguing possibilities can be reached without the integral element of the automobile: gas. In my mind, my education is the gas that will run my car that will take me to these places.

Why This Essay Bombed

The student might think that this concept of comparing life to a highway is quite inspired. In fact, she might have even talked about it with her friends and they might have been impressed. However, somewhere along the line she must have missed adult contact. This essay really just makes the applicant appear silly. She starts with an original idea but takes it too far in an overly simplified way. Being creative is good. But don't go overboard and end up with a laughable essay.

How To Avoid This Mistake

Have someone else read your essay. If you feel that maybe it is too creative or may border on being trite, ask what they think. Sometimes we just get too caught up in our own writing to make good judgments.

The Future Me

Scholarship organizations will often ask applicants where they see themselves in 10 years (or some other time in the not so distant future). Now we know what you're thinking—steady job, happily married, living in a nice house, two adorable children and dog named Spike. Stop right there, because this is your worst enemy. This idea is exactly what the 10,000 other applicants are thinking of writing about.

But wait a minute, this idea is *also* your best friend. You now have the perfect idea of what *not* to write about, and this information can prove quite useful when it comes to writing your own original essay. Here is an example of an essay that falls for this trap:

Ten Years From Now

Ten years from now, I see myself as a college graduate from a local private university. I will also have a steady job at a company for which I love to work. Hopefully I will be married, and, if I am, I'll probably have one or two kids. I plan to spend my free time with my family and maybe indulge in a few sporting events.

My job will probably be as an accountant, and I will give it my best. I'll like my job, because I've always liked to work with numbers. The only drawback will be that an accountant's salary will not be as much as I would desire to make. So I plan to achieve a state of wealth by investing in the stock market. By doing so, I will enable myself to retire at an early age.

In retirement I will continue to invest intelligently in the stock market so I can pay for my children's educations. I will travel the world with my family during the summers and donate to various charitable organizations.

My future will be a bright one provided that I get my own education. Ten years from now, the brightness will just be beginning to unveil, and I will be stepping into the happiest phase of my life.

Why This Essay Bombed

While this may be how the applicant truly feels it makes for one boring essay. It reflects the goals that almost every person has of being successful and happy, making the essay ordinary and unoriginal.

How To Avoid This Mistake

When you are asked where you see yourself in 10 years, focus on a single desire. You might write about an unfulfilled dream or a specific contribution that you hope to make. To make the essay more interesting, don't write about the future that nearly every other student will write about. Make your essay interesting by including your motivations, challenges, inspirations, rationale and expectations for your future.

My Life As Seen On TV

The average American spends dozens of hours watching television each week. It's not surprising then that entertainment from television, film and music finds its way into scholarship essays. While entertainment is an influence, it is a mistake to draw parallels to something when there really is little or no connection. Whatever topic you choose to write about should have a relationship to your life.

Liza

A movie I recently saw struck a heartfelt tone in my mind. I realized that the main character, Liza, was forced to struggle through circumstances similar to mine.

After losing her father in World War II, Liza's mother raised her as a single parent. Through the hardships, Liza's mother grew physically and mentally stronger because she knew she had to make sure that her daughter would be all right. Liza, however, did not appreciate her mother's efforts. Liza was an aspiring actress. Her favorite acting part during her senior year was playing Dorothy in *The Wizard of Oz*, the final play of her high school career.

On the night of the final performance, Liza's mother had a commitment that she could not afford to miss. Liza begged her mother to come in time to hear the last song--a reasonable request--and her mother lovingly promised that she would be there. Liza gave the greatest performance of her life that night and waited patiently for her mother to arrive, until the final song was about to be cued. At that point, Liza began to lose hope, and by the time the song was over she completely hated her mother. Liza waited around after the play until a police officer suddenly pulled up to the school to tell her that her mother had died at the hands of a drunk driver while on her way to the play. Devastated, Liza finally realized how much her mother really loved her.

The movie was especially touching because Liza lived her entire childhood trying to get away from her mother, but lived the remainder of her life appreciating how much her mother actually meant to her. My life story is similar to Liza's because I too am aspiring to be someone, except I aspire to be a psychologist. Also, I have been fortunate enough not to lose either of my parents, although my father has a strenuous work schedule, and I only see him in the mornings.

I have been inspired by this movie to appreciate the love, support and encouragement that my parents have provided for me in the past and which they continue to provide.

Why This Essay Bombed

Touching story, the movie that is. Not only is the writer's life nothing like that of Liza's, the inspiration the writer has received tells us nothing about the writer herself. This essay would work a lot better for someone who *has* suffered such tragedies and hardships.

How To Avoid This Mistake

As you are choosing a topic, it is fine to select one that shares a touching story, but this story should relate to your life. A good story is entertaining, but a better one gives insight into who you are.

Excuses, Excuses, Excuses

Nobody is perfect. We all make mistakes. Maybe you skipped a few too many 8 a.m. classes in freshman year. Perhaps you didn't put all of your effort into your science project. All of this is normal. However, what is not normal or useful is using your essay to explain past mistakes. Your essay should be used to highlight your strengths, not call the judges' attention to or make excuses for your shortcomings.

It's Not My Fault

I received horrible grades all throughout high school, but hardly any of them were due to my own actions. Let me explain: you'll notice that during freshman year I earned a 2.5 GPA. The reason for this is that I had just gone through a difficult move to a new city, the first time our family had relocated. It was hard for me to adjust to the new environment of living in a big city and I made few friends. Because of this, I had a very difficult time in all my classes, which, by the way, were chosen all by my overprotective mother.

Then, during sophomore year, I finally started to make some pretty good friends, but one day in the middle of October, my dog died. That devastated me. I took the SAT I that month and my results definitely reflect this loss. Throughout the year I couldn't recover from such a loss, because I had my dog since I was 5 years old.

Then came junior year. Emotionally, this was my worst year. I went through a terrible breakup with my girl-friend of five months in the middle of winter break. Since then, school has been in the way of my recovery, and I have performed poorly as a result. I tried taking the SAT I again, and my emotional weakness once again reflects my scores. APs and SAT IIs were no different. I joined the basketball team in the begin-ning of the year, but I was almost immediately cut.

Senior year I tried to make a comeback, but my GPA remained the same. This discouraged me because none of my friends believed I was intelligent. I tried to join clubs in the hopes that community involvement would cure my woes, but in fact the impersonality of clubs altogether discouraged me further so I haven't stayed in any.

Meanwhile, my family is running out of money. My dad has been laid off from his job for about six months now. I feel like the world is against me now, and I could really use this scholarship to help my college career, if I have one.

Why This Essay Bombed

What this essay does is call attention to the writer's deficiencies instead of his strengths. We all have things about ourselves that we are not proud of so why put them on display when trying to impress? Compounding this effect is that the student tries to avoid taking responsibility for his shortcomings by blaming everything and everyone else. If you are going to admit to a mistake then at least take responsibility for your actions.

How To Avoid This Mistake

Showcase your strengths in your essay. If you do need to reveal a weakness or shortcoming, explain how you have grown from this experience. We all make mistakes but what is important is that we learn from each of them. Whatever you do, don't avoid responsibility for your actions.

Complex Problem, Simple Solution

For some competitions, you may write about an issue of national or international importance. Scholarship committees ask these questions to find out what is important to you and to see your understanding of complex issues. It would seem fairly obvious that the biggest mistake you could make in writing this type of essay is to know nothing about the problem or to present a wholly unrealistic solution. Observe.

```
                    Nuclear Nightmare

Imagine a nuclear nightmare. Bombs exploding. Millions
of people vaporized. Entire cities destroyed. This is
the reality we face even after the Cold War has been
won.

The major problem is that nuclear weapons are all
around us. Nearly every country has them even if they
don't openly admit it. Worse yet is the fact that
anyone can easily build a bomb from plans posted on
various Internet websites. All you need is a small
quantity of uranium which is supposedly easily avail-
able at many hospitals and pharmacies.

The danger posed by nuclear weapons is all too real
and something must be done to combat this threat to
the world. I propose the following solution.
```

First, we must collect and destroy all nuclear weapons and sources of radiation. We need someone like the UN to collect all of the missiles and bombs and destroy them once and for all.

Then, we must erase all knowledge about building nuclear bombs. Since man cannot be trusted with this knowledge we need to destroy all plans and instructions on building bombs. While science is important this is one area of knowledge that it can do without. Once all plans and documents relating to nuclear bombs are destroyed it will take centuries for man to re-learn how to build them.

These two simple but decisive steps could rid the world of the threat of nuclear destruction. Once and for all we could all sleep at night without the fear of a nuclear nightmare.

Why This Essay Bombed

The problem with this essay is that the writer clearly does not have any knowledge of the problem of nuclear proliferation. Not only do some of the facts cited seem to have come from urban legends but there is no mention of the international aspect or diplomatic dimension of the problem. The second problem is the solution is entirely unrealistic. How do we go about collecting weapons? Is it even possible to remove knowledge once it is known? The writer assumes these are easy solutions when in fact they are extremely difficult, if not impossible.

How To Avoid This Mistake

Don't write about an issue without understanding it. You don't have to be an expert, but you should read about it and even discuss it with some of your teachers or professors. By speaking about the issues with others, you will gain a better understanding of the problem and this will also help you to generate innovative solutions. Your solutions do not have to be easy or even doable, but they do need to show some thought and understanding of the difficulty involved in solving any large national or international problem.

If possible, draw a connection between the issue and your own life. Have you taken action even on a personal level? Remember that the scholarship judges don't want a lecture on the issue as much as they want to learn about you and your ability to analyze a complex problem.

CHAPTER SEVEN

JUDGES' ROUNDTABLE: THE SCHOLARSHIP ESSAY

In this chapter:

■ Why the scholarship essay is so important

■ Common qualities of money-winning essays

■ How to avoid essay mistakes

Meet Your Scholarship Judges

In this second roundtable, judges and experts provide insight into the importance of scholarship essays and the qualities of those that win.

Q How important is the essay to winning a scholarship?

For many scholarship competitions the essay plays a vital role. It allows the selection committee to get to know you beyond your list of courses and achievements. In some competitions, the essay alone is the deciding factor that separates those who receive awards from those who don't.

Kimberly Hall
United Negro College Fund
"The essay is a very important piece of the application because it is often what the donor, who makes the final decision, will use to see the student's aspirations. It gives us a sense of who the student is and what they want to do with the money. It gives us a more complete picture of the student as a whole person as opposed to just a name."

Jacqui Love Marshall
Knight Ridder Minority Scholars Program
"In the end if we had to look at a student who had a little lower score and a little lower GPA but wrote an outstanding essay from the heart and had some experience or testimonials to back up their strengths, we'd be inclined to award the student with the strong essay. What really differentiates one applicant from another is a genuinely written essay."

Q What qualities make an essay powerful?

One of the keys to writing a powerful scholarship essay is to be honest and to write from the heart. The scholarship judges and experts have stressed that they can see through an essay that is not honest and that the best essays are about something for which the applicants are truly passionate.

Georgina Salguero
Hispanic Heritage Youth Awards
"We look at how you develop your thesis statement. What are you going to talk about and do you stick to those points? Do your paragraph structures make sense? We can tell how passionate you are for your subject by how you write. Don't just write that you want to attend college because you know you have to go to school. Instead, tell us why. Why do you want to go to college? What drives you? What gives you the strength to keep going?"

Shirley Kennedy Keller
American Association of School Administrators
"It's very important for them to be specific, to give specific examples of their leadership, special talents, obstacles or community service. The more specific they can be and the more they can back up their statements, the better they're going to fare in the judging process."

Kimberly Hall
United Negro College Fund
"Essays should be well developed in terms of the paragraph structure. The essay should have a definite purpose and direction. By the end of the essay we should know where you have started from and where you are heading. We want to see what you have dealt with and what your plan of action is. We also want to see where you see yourself in the future."

Trisha Bazemore
Coca-Cola Scholars Foundation
"You can tell when you read an essay if it's a real expression of something the student really cares about or if it was written just to impress. We intentionally don't provide students with instructions for the essay. We want to give each student the opportunity to be genuine."

Jacqui Love Marshall
Knight Ridder Minority Scholars Program
"Your essay needs to fit the scholarship. Sometimes when reading

an essay you get the feeling that the essay was written generically for 60 different scholarships and the author just substituted newspapering for engineering. If you want to win our scholarship your essay needs to tie into your involvement to the things we care about like the newspaper, photography or the sales or marketing side of the business."

Wanda Carroll
National Association of Secondary School Principals
"Go back to your basic English lessons and remember all that your English teacher taught. Make sure your essay is concise and there's a point to what you're writing."

Laura DiFiore
FreSch! Free Scholarship Search
"If you can make the reader laugh, cry or get angry, even when you're just writing about yourself, you've already won half the game. That's the bottom line. Get an emotional response out of the reader."

 # What common mistakes do students make on the essay?

As you're writing your essay, it's important to know what works. But sometimes it can be even more helpful to know what doesn't work. By knowing what mistakes kill an otherwise good essay you can avoid them in your own writing. After having read hundreds or even thousands of essays, our panel has encountered many common mistakes that students make in their scholarship essays.

Kimberly Hall
United Negro College Fund
"Some students write their essays about the difficulties that they have faced but do so in a negative way and don't explain how they've overcome the difficulties. I would recommend that students present a positive light. Here are some of the challenges that I've had to overcome and here is how I did it. Stay positive."

Tracey Wong Briggs
All-USA Academic Teams
"There are some students who have outstanding biographical information, but when you read the essay all they've done is recount the facts that are in their application form. We want you to use the essay to go deeper and beyond what is listed in your application. We lose very good nominees that way. They just don't give you a clear idea of who they are beyond the basic facts."

Mario A. De Anda
Hispanic Scholarship Fund
"One of the common mistakes is that they use the same personal statement for many scholarships. They even forget to change the name of the scholarship they are applying to. We encourage students to make sure they write a personal statement specifically for the program."

Laura DiFiore
FreSch! Free Scholarship Search
"A huge mistake is what I call the crush, when we're getting 40 to 50 percent of our applications in the last three days. I think a lot of students would be better off if they didn't apply in the last two weeks before the deadline. The ones rushing to get in by the deadline would probably be better off spending more time on their essays and applying next year."

Wanda Carroll
National Association of Secondary School Principals
"Spelling. You should use your computer's spell check. We wouldn't disqualify an applicant solely on spelling, but the committee does see the mistakes and it does distract from the quality of the essay. If they had a choice between two equally well-written essays, they would choose the essay without spelling errors."

Leah Carroll
U.C. Berkeley Haas Scholars Program
"The most common error I run into is people who are trying to say what the foundation wants to hear. It ends up sounding inauthentic. I tell students to write as if they are trying to explain something to a friend. Just write from the heart. They seem to always come out better that way. Another mistake is that students, at Ber-

keley in particular, often sell themselves short. You should not be afraid to call attention to all of your achievements."

Michael Darne
Wiredscholar
"When approaching the essay a lot of students are eager to dump a huge laundry list of achievements–a list of everything that they've done. But what scholarship providers are looking for is to get an understanding of who this person is and where they're going in life. They don't just want a list of accomplishments. If you can paint some picture of yourself, where you're going and how you're going to get there, you're going to be in a much better situation."

Georgina Salguero
Hispanic Heritage Youth Awards
"We're not giving the award to the best sob story. We're not looking for someone who can write the best woe is me story. Please don't give us this kind of essay."

Participating Judges & Experts

Trisha Bazemore, Program Assistant, Coca-Cola Scholars Foundation

Tracey Wong Briggs, Coordinator, *USA Today* All-USA Academic and Teacher Teams

Leah Carroll, Coordinator, U.C. Berkeley Haas Scholars Program and former program coordinator, U.C. Berkeley Scholarship Connection

Wanda Carroll, Program Manager, National Association of Secondary School Principals

Michael Darne, Director of Business Development, Wiredscholar, the website of Sallie Mae

Mario A. De Anda, Director of Scholarship Programs, Hispanic Scholarship Fund

Laura DiFiore, Founder, FreSch! Free Scholarship Search Let's Get Creative Short Story and Poetry Scholarship Contest

Kimberly Hall, Peer Program Manager, United Negro College Fund

Shirley Kennedy Keller, Program Director, American Association of School Administrators, which administers the Discover Card Tribute Award Scholarship

Jacqui Love Marshall, Vice President of Human Resources, Diversity and Development, Knight Ridder Minority Scholars Program

Georgina Salguero, Senior Manager, Programs and Events, Hispanic Heritage Youth Awards

WINNING INTERVIEW STRATEGIES

In this chapter:

■ **The two types of interviews**

■ **How to ace the interview**

■ **Who are the interviewers**

■ **How to dress and act**

■ **What to do if you have a disaster interview**

Face-To-Face With The Interview

The good news is that if you need to do an interview for a scholarship, you are probably a serious contender. The bad news may be that you will now undergo the nerve-wracking scrutiny of an interview with one or more scholarship judges. If you are starting to feel your palms moisten or a sinking feeling in your stomach, you are not alone.

The best way to overcome your fear of the interview is to know exactly what to expect and be prepared for the questions you might be asked. In this chapter, we discuss what scholarship interviewers are looking for in your answers as well as give you some strategies on how to prepare.

Many students wonder why they have to do an interview in the first place. While some scholarships are awarded solely based on your written application, many scholarship committees like to perform face-to-face interviews to make the final decision. Particularly, if the scholarship is for a significant amount of money, the selection committee wants to be sure to give it to the most deserving student possible.

Having sat on both sides of the interview table, we can attest to the fact that an interview can shed significant insight on an applicant. Before we discuss how to make the most of your interview, let's cover the two situations you may face.

Two Types Of Interviews

There are basically two types of interviews: 1) friendly and 2) less than friendly or even hostile. The friendly interview is fairly low key with the scholarship judges asking easy to answer questions and trying to get to know you better. While most interviews fall into the friendly camp, others especially for highly competitive and prestigious awards such as the Rhodes or Truman are far less pleasant. In these interviews the scholarship judges want to test you to see how you react to stressful and difficult questions. A hostile interview creates an environment for the judges to be able to evaluate how you react to pressure.

Whenever you encounter hostile judges or interview situations, keep in mind that they are not trying to personally attack you or diminish your accomplishments but are observing how you respond to the situation. Also, keep in mind that they will act the same toward all applicants.

How To Ace Your Interview – Friendly Or Hostile

Regardless of the type of interview you encounter the keys to success are the same. First, remember that scholarship interviewers are real people. This is especially true for hostile situations where you may have to fight your feelings of anger or frustration with the interviewer. Your goal is to create as engaging a conversation as possible. This means you can't give short, one-sentence answers and you certainly should not be afraid to ask questions. Most interviewers enjoy conversations over interrogations.

The second key to the interview is to practice. The more you practice interviewing, the easier and more natural your answers will be. Practice can take the form of asking and answering your own questions out loud or finding someone to conduct a mock interview. Consider taping your mock interview so you can review your technique. Having someone simulate a hostile interview is very good practice and will give you a tremendous edge over applicants who have not experienced this yet.

Transform An Interrogation Into A Conversation

The reason most people volunteer to be scholarship judges is because they are passionate about the organization or award they are supporting. Being an interviewer is also hard work. In most cases, interviewers have a few questions to begin with but then hope the interviewee can help carry the conversation and direct it into other interesting areas. In fact, it is very difficult to interview an applicant who quickly and succinctly answers the questions but offers nothing else to move the conversation forward.

As an interviewee you are an essential part of determining where the conversation goes and whether or not it is easy or difficult for the interviewers. Your job is to supply the interviewers not only with complete answers but also with information that leads to other interesting topics of conversation.

It helps to know something about your interviewers. One thing you know is that they care about their organization. They may be members of the organization or long-time supporters. The more you learn about the organization and its membership the better idea you'll have about your interviewers and what interests them.

This knowledge is useful in helping you choose how to answer questions that require you to highlight a specific area of your life or achievements, topics to avoid and questions you should ask.

Before every interview, do your homework on the award and the awarding organization, which includes knowing the following:

Purpose of the scholarship. What is the organization hoping to accomplish by awarding the scholarship? Whether it's promoting students to enter a certain career, encouraging a hobby or interest or rewarding students for leadership, every scholarship has a mission. By understanding why the organization is giving away the money, you can share with interviewers how you meet their priorities.

Criteria for selecting the winner. From the scholarship materials, you can get a reasonable idea of what the selection committee is looking for when choosing the winner. From the kinds of information they request in the application to the topic of the essay question, each piece is a clue about what is important to the scholarship committee.

Background of the awarding organization. Do a little digging on the organization itself. Check out its website or publications. Attend a meeting or speak with a member. From this detective work, you will get a better idea of who the organization's members are and what they are trying to achieve. Knowing something about the organization will also prevent you from making obvious blunders during the interview.

Once you've done your detective work, think about how the information can help you. Let's take a look at one piece of information you might learn. Imagine you discovered that the organi-

Advice From A Rhodes Scholar
Kristin N. Javaras, Oxford University

The interview is one of last hurdles to becoming a prestigious Rhodes Scholar. Kristin, who is working on a doctorate in statistics at Oxford University, says about interviews, "The best advice I can offer is to be yourself, as trite as that may sound."

But what happens when you are stumped for an answer? "If you just don't know the answer to a question, don't be afraid to admit it," advises Kristin.

Regarding the type of questions that she was asked, Kristin recalls, "Almost every question was at least tangentially and often directly related to topics and experiences mentioned in my personal statement or included in my list of activities and jobs."

zation you are applying to values leadership. In addition, you discover from reading the organization's website that all of its members are invited to join only if they have led large companies. Knowing this you could guess that your interviewers will probably be business leaders and will be most impressed if you highlight your leadership and entrepreneurial activities. If asked about your greatest achievement you can now insightfully highlight being president of your school's business club over anything else.

Knowing something about your interviewers beforehand will also help you think of appropriate and engaging questions. Most interviewers allow time for you to ask a few questions toward the end of the interview. By asking intelligent questions (i.e., not the ones that can be answered by simply reading the group's website), you will hopefully be able to touch upon something the interviewer really cares about that will lead to further conversation.

Going back to our example, you might ask a question such as, "As the president of the business club one of our greatest challenges has been to get funding from businesses for new projects and ideas. What advice do you have for young business people to secure seed money from established businesses?"

This question not only demonstrates that you know the background of your interviewers but also poses a question that they can answer with their expertise, and it could start a new conversation about how to fund a business idea.

You Are Not The Center Of The Universe

Despite what you think, you are not the center of the universe—at least not yet! Therefore, in the interview you need to keep it interactive by not just focusing on yourself.

This can be accomplished by asking questions and engaging in a two-way conversation. If you don't ask any questions, it will appear that you are not attentive or you haven't put much thought into your interview. Beforehand, develop a list of questions you may want to ask. Of course you don't have to ask all of your questions, but be prepared to ask a few.

To get you started, we've developed some suggestions. Adapt these questions to the specific scholarship you are applying for, and personalize them.

- How did you get involved with this organization?
- How did you enter this field? What was your motivation for entering this field?
- Who were your mentors? Heroes?
- What do you think is the most exciting things about this field?
- What professional advice do you have?
- What do you see as the greatest challenges?
- What do you think will be the greatest advancements in the next 10 years?
- What effect do you think technology will have on this field?

Ultimately, the more interaction you have and the more you engage the interviewers the better their impression of you. You want to leave them with the feeling that you are a polite and intelligent person who is as interested in what they have to say as in what you do.

Dress & Act The Part

Studies have shown than in speeches, the audience remembers what you look like and how you sound more than what you actu-

---

The Group Interview
Key Strategies

So it's you on one side of the table and a panel of six on the other side. It's certainly not the most natural way to have a conversation. How do you stay calm when you are interviewed by a council of judges? Here's how:

Think of the group as individuals. Instead of thinking it's you versus the team, think of each of the interviewers as an individual. Try to connect with each separately.

Try to get everyone's name if you can. Have a piece of paper to jot down everyone's name and role so that you can refer to them in the conversation and be able to target your answers to appeal to each of the constituents. For example, if you are interviewing with a panel of employees from a company and you know that Sue works in accounting while Joe works in human resources, you can speak about your analytical skills to appeal to Sue and your people skills to appeal to Joe.

Make eye contact. Look into the eyes of each of the panelists. Don't stare, but show them that you are confident. Be careful not to focus on only one or two panelists.

Respect the hierarchy. You may find that there is a leader in the group like the scholarship chair or the CEO of the company. Pay a little more attention to stroke the ego of the head. A little kissing up never hurt anyone.

Try to include everyone. In any group situation, there is usually one or two more vocal members who take the lead. Don't focus all of your attention only on the loud ones. Spread your attention as evenly as possible.

ally say. While it may seem unimportant, your presentation style and presence are probably more significant than you think.

Think about the delivery of your answers and keep the following points in mind.

Sit up straight. During interviews, you should not slouch. Sitting up straight conveys confidence, strength and intelligence. It communicates that you are interested in the conversation.

Speak in a positive tone of voice. One thing that keeps interviewers engaged is your tone. Make sure to speak in a positive one. This will not only maintain your interviewers' interest but will also suggest that you have an optimistic outlook toward life.

Don't be monotonous. Speaking at the same rate and tone of voice without variation is a good way to give your interviewers very heavy eyelids. Tape record yourself and pay attention to your tone of voice. There should be a natural variation in your timbre.

Speak at a natural pace. If you're like most people, the more nervous you are the faster you speak. Combat this by speaking on the slower side of your natural pace. If during your interview you think you are speaking too slowly, in reality you are speaking at just the right pace.

Make natural gestures. Let your hands and face convey action and emotions. Use them as tools to illustrate anecdotes and punctuate important points.

Make eye contact. Eye contact engages interviewers and conveys self-assurance and honesty. If it is a group interview, make eye contact with all of your interviewers—don't just focus on one. Maintaining good eye contact can be difficult, but just imagine little dollar signs in your interviewers' eyes and you shouldn't have any trouble. Ka-ching!

Smile. There's nothing more depressing than having a conversation with someone who never smiles. Don't smile nonstop, but show some teeth at least once in a while.

Dress appropriately. This means business attire. No-no's include: caps, bare midriffs, short skirts or shorts, open-toe shoes and wrinkles. Think about covering obtrusive tattoos or removing extra ear/nose/tongue/eyebrow rings. Don't dress so formally that you feel uncomfortable, but dress nicely. It may not seem fair, but your dress will affect the impression you make and influence the judgment of the committee.

If you use these tips, you will have a flawless look and sound to match what you're saying. All of these attributes together create a powerful portrait of who you are. Remember that not all of these things come naturally, so you'll need to practice before they become unconscious actions.

What It's Like To Be An Interviewer
Rotary International Ambassadorial Scholarships

Selection committees are typically composed of volunteers who sign up for a long day of interviews. By understanding their role, you can see the importance of interacting with them, keeping their attention and giving them a reason to want to listen to what you have to say.

Each year the selection committee for Rotary International in the San Francisco Bay Area interviews about 15 applicants. The six or seven selection committee members, Rotarians and previous scholarship winners start the day at 8:30 a.m. and end at 6 p.m., with 45 minutes for lunch and a couple of stretch breaks. They spend about 30 minutes with each applicant.

"After the interview, we score and go to the next one," says Russ Hobbs, district scholarship chairman.

Surprisingly, Hobbs says that there is no advantage to interviewing earlier in the day than later. Still, to be fair, they schedule the interviews randomly instead of alphabetically. Despite the long day Rotary has little trouble finding volunteers, he says, "Because the applicants are such phenomenally interesting people."

How To Make Practice Into Perfect

The best way to prepare for an interview is to do a dress rehearsal before the real thing. This allows you to run through answering questions you might be asked, practice honing your demeanor and feel more comfortable when it comes time for the actual interview. Force yourself to set aside some time to run through a practice session at least once. Here's how:

Find mock interviewers. Bribe or coerce a friend or family member to be your mock interviewer. Parents, teachers or professors make great interviewers.

Prep your mock interviewers. Give them questions from the next chapter to start with and also ask them to think of some of their own. Share with them what areas of your presentation you are trying to improve so that they can pay attention and give you constructive feedback. For example, if you know that you fidget during the interview ask them to pay special attention to your posture and movements.

Capture yourself on tape. If you have a tape recorder or camcorder, set it up to tape yourself so that you can review your mock interview. Position the camera behind your interviewer so you can observe how you appear from the right perspective.

Get feedback. After you are finished, get constructive criticism from your mock interviewer. Find out what you did well and what you need to work on. What were the best parts of the interview? Which of your answers were strong, and which were weak? When did you capture or lose your mock interviewer's attention? Was your conversation one-way or two-way?

Review the tape. If you can, watch or listen with your mock interviewer so you can get additional feedback. Listen carefully to how you answer questions so you can improve on them. Pay attention to your tone of voice. Watch your body language to see what it communicates.

Do it again. If you have the time and your mock interviewer has the energy or you can find another one, do a second interview. If you can't find anyone, do it solo. Practice your answers, and focus on making some of the weaker ones more interesting.

The bottom line is the more you practice, the better you'll do.

The Long-Distance Interview

Interviewing over the telephone is a real challenge. While most interviews are held in person, sometimes you just can't meet face-to-face. When this happens, the telephone is the only option. The most difficult aspect is that you can't judge the reactions of your interviewers. You have no idea if what you are saying is making them smile or frown. While there is no way to overcome the inherent disadvantage of a phone interview, here are some tips that should help to bridge the distance:

Find a quiet place. You want to do the interview in a place where you won't be interrupted. You need to be able to pay full attention to the conversation you are having.

Know who's on the other end of the line. You may interview with a panel of people. Write down each of their names and positions when they first introduce themselves to you. They will be impressed when you are able to respond to them individually and thank each of them by name.

Use notes from your practice interviews. One of the advantages of doing an interview over the telephone is that you can refer to notes. Take advantage of this.

Look and sound like you would in person. Pretend your interviewers are in the room with you, and use the same gestures and facial expressions that you would if you were meeting in person. It may sound strange, but your interviewers will actually be able to hear through your voice when you are smiling, when you are paying attention and when you are enthusiastic about what you're saying. Don't do your interview lying down in your bed or slouched back in a recliner.

Don't use a speaker phone, cordless phone or cell phone. Speaker phones often echo and pick up distracting noise. Cordless

The Hostile Interview
U.C. Berkeley & Truman Scholarship Winners

In some scholarship competitions, particularly ones for prestigious awards like the Rhodes, Marshall or Truman, the interviews are designed to challenge you. To do well you need to prepare and have the right mindset for these challenging interviews. —Gen and Kelly

During his interview to become a Truman Scholar, one of the eight panelists asked Brian C. Babcock to name a good funny novel he had recently read. Brian hadn't read a humorous novel recently, but he did have a children's book that he thought was funny.

He started to say, "It's not a novel, but…" and before he finished the interviewer interrupted him to say, "No, I want a novel."

The sentiment in most scholarship interviews is friendly and cordial. But for some competitions, particularly the prestigious ones with fierce national competition, the setting is often challenging and even adversarial.

"There's a kind of devil's advocate interviewing style for these competitions. The phrasing and tone is more antagonistic," says Leah Carroll, coordinator of U.C. Berkeley's Haas Scholars Program and former program coordinator of the university's Scholarship Connection office, which assists students who are applying for awards.

She coaches students to view these kinds of interviews as "intellectual sparring," and advises them to "practice interviews with friends and to tell their friends to be mean."

Donald H. Matsuda, Jr. experienced this intellectual sparring first hand. A student at Stanford University, Matsuda is also a Truman Scholar. The panel challenged his policy plan on health care for children asking why they should "continue to waste millions of our federal budget to help this situation that has no clear cut solution."

Donald was also asked to define music. The panel gave him the option of defining it or singing a definition. He chose to define it.

Brian's contributions reflect his own opinions, not those of the U.S. military.

He said, "I see music as the ultimate way a person can express himself. I chose not to sing, which is why I think I won the Truman."

A student at the U.S. Military Academy, Brian applied for the award to receive a master's in foreign service and history and certificate in Russian area studies. In his interview, the selection committee asked Brian questions about gays in the Boy Scouts, an example of bad leadership and why he wanted to work in public service instead of make millions of dollars.

They challenged his choice of topic for his essay, asking why he chose as an example of leadership when he led one other person instead of when he led many. He answered, "If you can't lead one person how can you expect to lead a group?"

And, they questioned his grades, which weren't perfect but still high. He says, "I explained that to me it was more important to get the breadth of knowledge and take the classes while I have the time and it's free. I take as much as I can handle. If that means that my grades slip from a 3.9 to a 3.75 so be it."

Besides preparing for the interview, what may have helped Brian was his frame of mind. He says, "I didn't have an interview. I had a talk with eight people around the table."

and cell phones can generate static, and the battery can die at the worst possible moment.

Turn off call waiting. Nothing is more annoying than hearing the call waiting beep while you are trying to focus and deliver an important thought. (And, this may sound obvious, but don't click over to take a second call during the interview.)

The Disaster Interview

Even if you do your interview homework and diligently practice mock interviewing, you may still find that you and your interviewer just don't connect or that you just don't seem to have the right answers. If you spend some time preparing, this is very unlikely. Interviewers are not trying to trick you or make you feel bad. They are simply trying to find out more about you and your fit with the award. Still, if you think that you've bombed, here are some things to keep in mind:

Avoid "should have," "would have," "could have." Don't replay the interview in your head again and again, thinking of all the things you "should have" said. It's too easy to look back and have the best answers. Instead, use what you've learned to avoid making the same mistakes in your next interview.

There are no right answers. Remember that in reality there are no right answers. Your answers may have not been perfect, but that doesn't mean they were wrong. There are countless ways to answer the same question.

The toughest judge is you. Realize that you are your own greatest critic. While you may think that you completely bombed an interview, your interviewer will most likely not have as harsh an opinion.

Post-Interview

After you complete your interviews, follow up with a thank you note. Remember that interviewers are typically volunteers and have made the time to meet with you. If you feel that there is very important information that you forgot to share in your interview, mention it briefly in your thank you note. If not, a simple thank you will suffice.

Make Sure You Make Your Point
Jason Morimoto, State Farm Exceptional Student

"I have been involved in practically every type of interview whether it be a single interviewer, a panel or a phone interview.

"The toughest by far are the phone interviews because the scholarship committee cannot physically see who you are and your facial expressions.

"I personally prefer the panel interviews because it gives you a chance to make a strong impression on multiple people. I have found great success with panels.

"However, no matter what the format of the interview, the most important thing is to make sure that you get across your main strengths. If they do not ask you directly, try to weave it in with a related story or tie it in as a closing statement. You always want to give the most information possible to the interviewers so that they can understand your uniqueness as a person."

CHAPTER NINE

INTERVIEW
QUESTION &
ANSWER
EXAMPLES

In this chapter:

■ See what makes a great answer

■ Questions you'll likely face in your scholarship interview

■ Interview tips from winners

Giving The Right Answers

Imagine that your professor gave you the questions to an exam before you took it. Your score would certainly be higher. In this chapter we give you precisely this advantage by sharing the questions you're likely to be asked in your scholarship interviews. Plus, we show you examples of how to answer. You will be a fly on the wall, observing a typical scholarship interview.

Before the preview, we have a couple of caveats. Remember that these questions and answers are meant to be examples. They are not the only acceptable way to answer a question. In fact, there are innumerable ways to answer each question successfully.

Also, since your background and achievements are different, your answers will inevitably be different too. Don't focus on the specific details of the answers. Instead, look at the overall message and impression that each answer conveys.

The comments that follow each question are based on interviews with actual scholarship judges as well as our own experience in competing for scholarships. To get the most out of this chapter, we suggest that you read a question first and then pause to think about how you would answer it. Then read the response and comments. Keeping the comments in mind, analyze how the judges might react to your response. Be tough on yourself and think of ways to strengthen your answers. If your parents or friends are helping you practice interviewing, ask them to also read through a couple of the questions and answers to get a better idea of what kind of questions to ask and what to look for in responses.

Achievements & Leadership Questions

Q: **What achievement are you the most proud of?**

> A: This may not seem like an achievement to many people, but it is for me. Last year I learned how to swim. Ever since I can remember I've had a grave fear of the water. Anything above knee level was a frightening ex-

perience. Last year my little brother fell into a pool and had to be rescued by the lifeguard. As I stood by not able to help, I realized that I needed to learn to swim. Twice a week I went to swimming lessons. It was kind of embarrassing to be in a swimming class with elementary school students but I was determined to learn. It took an entire class for me to feel comfortable walking in the water up to my neck, but after eight weeks of lessons, I could actually swim several laps. I never thought that I could learn. I'm proud of this accomplishment not because it was difficult to learn but because of the huge fear I had to face and overcome to learn it.

A: Unlike other schools, ours never had a debate team. Because I want to be an attorney, I wanted to get practice in debating so I decided to form a team. None of the teachers at my school had the time to be the faculty adviser so I contacted local attorneys in the yellow pages. I finally found one who despite her busy schedule volunteered to help us. I recruited 12 other students to join and became the team captain. In our first year we made it to the district competition and won several rounds. For me this was my biggest accomplishment especially since now we have a core group of debaters who will continue the team after I graduate.

Comments

This is a challenging question because in addition to selecting and describing an accomplishment, you need to put it into context and explain its significance. The first answer vividly illustrates how this student overcomes his fears to learn how to swim. Everyone has something that they are deathly afraid of, and it is likely that the judges can easily relate to this accomplishment. Notice how the answer reveals why the student decided to face his fear of swimming and gives enough detail to create a mental picture. There is also a nice element of humor in the story that makes you smile.

The second answer is an excellent example of how to highlight an impressive achievement. While the scholarship judges may notice that this student is the founder of her school's debate team in the application, this answer underscores just how difficult it was to start the team. It also reveals the student's desire to be an attorney. The applicant ends nicely by emphasizing how her achievement has affected others and will continue to make a positive impact on the lives of her fellow students.

Q: **How have you been a leader or displayed leadership?**

A: I am the chair of my dorm committee. Our dorm committee consists of six officers who I oversee and our dorm has 500 student residents. My responsibilities include planning the orientation for new students, organizing social activities and directing our dorm's annual charity event. It's a challenge to get students motivated for a special event because there are so many other ways that they can spend their time. I am most proud of the way that I have been able to mobilize the students in our dorm to support our annual charity event, the bowl-a-thon for lung cancer research. To make this event a success I knew that I needed the help of others in our dorm. I recruited and trained hall representatives to personally contact all 500 students in our dorm and encourage them to participate in the bowl-a-thon. In the end over 50 percent of the students participated. We had a higher participation rate and donation level than any other dorm at our school.

A: This year I organized an event to collect toys for underprivileged children. I started by writing an article for the school newspaper to raise awareness and get students to donate toys. I had volunteers who also went to local businesses and asked for donations as well as a group that decided which families in our town would receive the toys. The toy drive was a huge success. We were able to provide toys to over 200 families and solicited donations from over 50 local businesses.

Comments

What's notable about both of these answers is that the applicants don't just list off a bunch of titles and positions. Instead the students focus on one specific leadership position or activity and

> # Tip #1 From A Scholarship Winner
> ## Elisa Tatiana Juárez, Brown University
>
> "Be proud of what you've done. Don't be falsely modest, but also make sure that you don't give the impression of being egotistical. The ability to talk positively about my accomplishments took me a long time to learn. I was afraid showing people what I've done would make me sound too conceited. Always remember that the judges want to know why they should pick you. Show them."

give enough detail to show the depth of their commitment. Citing concrete accomplishments like getting half of her dorm to participate or giving toys to over 200 familiars also helps judges to better gauge the significance of each achievement. The second answer illustrates that you don't have to hold an official title or elected position in order to show leadership. This applicant, who does not hold an elected position, is still able to answer this question impressively by describing how she has organized an event. You can certainly be a leader and motivator even if you don't have an official title.

Personal Questions

Q: What is your greatest strength and weakness?

A: One of my strengths is my ability to lead. For example, at my school we didn't have a recycling program. The janitors wouldn't pick up the paper for recycling because it wasn't in their contracts. I met with our principal to discuss the problem, but he said the school didn't have the budget to pay for a recycling program. So I started a program myself. I got donations to buy bins to put in each of the classrooms and went to each class to make a speech to get volunteers to collect the papers for recycling. Every month, I gathered the volunteers for a meeting to discuss any changes or problems.

One of my weaknesses is impatience. I get frustrated when I see a problem but nothing is happening to fix it.

I like to see people working toward solutions. I got very frustrated when I first found out that there was no recycling program at my school and especially when the janitors said they wouldn't pick up the recycling even though I thought it didn't require that much extra work. But I guess it was this frustration that led me to do something about it.

A: My strength is in math. Ever since elementary school I have been talented in math. In school, when everyone else was struggling with algebra and geometry, I didn't have any trouble. I just imagined the problems in my head, visualizing the pyramids, spheres and cones. My math teacher even asked me to grade homework assignments. And I've represented our school each year for the county math competition.

My weakness is creative writing. I think because of the way that my mind works, it can be difficult to write creative essays. This is one of the reasons why last summer I took a creative writing class, and it really helped. The instructor had us pretend to be another person in the class and write from the other person's perspective. We also went outside and imagined being the grass, trees and sun. I never thought like that before and it's really opened up my mind to some new possibilities. This is one area that I know I need to work on to improve.

Comments

It's easy to say that your strength is that you work hard. But what will really prove to the judges that you work hard is an example. Use an example to illustrate your strength so that the judges can see what you mean. It's not enough to say that your strength is leadership. How have you led? What kind of results have come from your leadership? Why do you do it? Both of these strength answers are good in giving complete examples. But more importantly they also help to contrast and balance the weakness. In the second response where the applicant admits to not being a skilled creative writer, this not only reveals an honest flaw but also gives him an opportunity to show what action he has taken to improve. There is nothing wrong with acknowledging a weakness, but it is

Misinterpreting The Judges
Silver Knight Scholarship Winner

It's tempting to try to read the judges during your scholarship interview. You might think that the longer the interview or the more involved the selection committee gets, the better your performance. Unfortunately, it's very hard to accurately interpret the thoughts of others. When she interviewed for the Silver Knight scholarship, Elisa Tatiana Juárez was scared. After all, the Silver Knight award is a highly competitive program and is given to only 14 of the top students in Miami-Dade County.

Elisa had been on the other side of the interview table before as an interviewer so she thought she had a good sense of how judges react when they are really interested in a candidate.

"I thought that you could tell what the judges think of you by their responses," she says.

In the interview, Elisa described the STARS (Students and Teachers Advocating Research Science) program that she started at the Miami Museum of Science to provide opportunities for minority and economically disadvantaged students in the sciences. During her interview, she was disappointed that the judges seemed too enthusiastic about her work to the point that she thought they were faking their level of interest.

"In my interview, they were too encouraging," she says. "My image was they thought, `Good luck, but try again next year.'"

Thankfully, her interpretation of their reactions was completely opposite from reality and she won the award.

very impressive to see that you are also taking steps to transform that weakness into a strength.

Q: Who is a role model for you?

A: Oprah Winfrey. I admire Oprah not because of her wealth but because through sheer determination and hard work she has built one of the largest media companies in the country. I am inspired by people like Oprah who didn't inherit wealth or fame but who built it on their own by setting goals and working hard to achieve them. She is also motivating because she has chosen to do what she wanted to do, not necessarily what was seen as the most popular thing to do. For example, instead of making her talk show about sex and violence, she's taken a different route to make it about the positive things in life. I also want to live my life by what I think is right, even if that is at odds with what the majority feel I should do.

A: My father is my role model. He has taught me to endure difficult times with resolve. I always knew that my father didn't make a lot of money at his job and that our family's finances were stretched. But I only recently learned how stretched our finances were. There were points where my parents weren't sure how they were going to pay the bills. But looking at my father, you would never detect the stress that he was under. He always made sure that we kids had everything that we needed. We didn't have the brightest or newest things, but we were always cared for. I remember one Christmas when I was 12. My friends received the newest "in" toys for Christmas while I received a wooden car and airplane that my father had made. I still have those toys and plan to give them to my kids someday. That is what I admire about my father and hope that in the face of adversity I too can be as calm and innovative as he is.

Comments

When judges ask you this question, their intent is to learn something about you through your choice of whom you admire. If you just say that your role model is golfing superstar Tiger Woods but offer no explanation why, you aren't sharing much about yourself. The judges won't know if Tiger is your role model because he's a good golfer, a Stanford graduate or something else. Both of these answers give specific reasons why the applicants idolize these people, and both support their choice with concrete and memorable examples. No matter whom you choose as your hero, be sure to know enough about them to explain what specifically you want to emulate. Also, know their shortcomings since you may be asked about that as a follow-up question.

Q: What is your favorite book?

A: *Les Miserables* by Victor Hugo. When we were first assigned to read this book, it was pretty daunting. But as I started reading, I couldn't put it down. I became consumed with the characters, feeling their emotions. The book took me through the low points of Jean Valjean's arrests and the high point of his final release. Throughout, the book made me think about the line between right and wrong and whether or not someone who was wrong in the past could make up for his or her mistakes to experience true freedom. It really made me think about the ethics I live by and about the mistakes I've made in the past. It also inspired me to be more forgiving of people with whom I've had disagreements.

A: *The Day Lincoln Was Shot* by Jim Bishop. This book chronicles the last 24 hours of Lincoln's life from the perspective of the assassins and the government officials who were the target of the assassination plot. I normally don't get drawn into history books, but this one was an exception because the detail allowed me to imagine everything that was happening and I felt like I was actually there. After reading the book, I took a drive to Washington, D.C., to see the Ford Theater and the boarding house where Lincoln died. I could almost see Booth approaching the President from behind and the doctors working on the President in vain. This book brought history alive for me, and I have a whole new interest in the American presidency.

Comments

Neither of these answers are book reports—which is good since the judges are not asking for a summary of the book. What the judges want to learn is who you are through your selection of a book and why you say it is important. Both of these answers show how the book affected the reader. When you are thinking about which book you would choose, ask yourself if your choice of book made you think differently or compelled you to take action. Ask yourself what specifically made you relate to a character. Also, don't feel that you have to select a classic. It's fine to say that your favorite book is *Charlotte's Web* or *Green Eggs and Ham.* What's important is not your selection of the book but why it is meaningful to you.

Why You Deserve To Win Questions

Q: **Why do you think you deserve to win this scholarship?**

A: I believe that by giving this award you are trying to help students who show academic promise and who will contribute to the community. Since my first day of school, my parents have instilled in me a commitment to academics, and I have a nearly perfect academic record. I am on track to graduating with highest honors. I have also been contributing to my community for many years. I started a program to provide books for a local elementary school's library. By using funds from book fairs, I increased the number of books at the elementary school from 500 to 2,500. My commitment to learning and public service are two things that I believe very strongly in and will continue throughout my life.

A: This award is meant to assist students who are interested in business. I have been an entrepreneur since I was a kid and convinced my parents that I could organize a neighborhood-wide garage sale. We raised several hundred dollars that way. In school, I started a tutor-matching business. Students let me know what kind of help they needed, and I matched them to an appropriate tutor. Through ventures like this I've learned the value of marketing, building relationships and having a business plan. I'm planning on majoring in business and have a business internship lined up this summer. Ultimately I would like to be a professor at a business school so that I can continue to learn and pass on to others the knowledge and skills that will make them successful business people.

Comments

Both of these applicants do a good job of focusing on the purpose of the award to clearly explain how their background and achievements fulfill this purpose. It's important to address how you meet the mission of the award or the awarding organization. Be as specific as possible. Don't just say that you should win the scholarship because you are a good student. Give details and examples to support what you say.

Q: What would winning this scholarship mean to you?

A: For me, winning this scholarship could mean the difference between going to college or working full-time. Without this award, I will need to work for a couple years to save up enough money to go to college. I've been accepted to the college that I want to go to, but I simply don't have the money to pay for it. My parents didn't go to college, and I'll be the first. And I will go. The question is whether it will be now or in a couple years.

A: My parents have spent the last 17 years taking care of me. Now I have a chance to do something to help them by winning scholarships. I feel that I owe it to my parents to try as best I can to help pay for my education. Winning this award would help to reduce their burden and help me to fulfill my goal of repaying my parents for all that they have done for me.

A: While I plan to work during the school year to earn money, winning this scholarship would mean that I could work fewer hours. Instead of working 20 hours a week, I could work only 10 hours and spend my extra time on my studies. It's been tough to balance working with my studies, and winning this award would help immensely.

Comments

Impact is important. Scholarship committees are trying to get the maximum benefit from their award. If the award will make the difference between you being able to attend a college or not, say so. The judges will understand that this award is more meaningful to you than to a student who already has a way to pay for his or her education. But be careful not to unload all of the challenges you face in the form of a sob story. Remember that many of the other applicants also have financial need.

Education & College Questions

Q: Why is education important to you?

A: My dream is to work in the medical field. I want a job that makes me personally satisfied. An important part of this is being able to help people on a daily basis. I also know that I need to be challenged to be happy. So the medical profession is a perfect match since it allows me to contribute to society while working in an intellectually challenging environment. This past summer I volunteered at our county hospital and worked closely with a neurologist. What intrigued me was how he was able to look at a set of symptoms and test results and figure out what was wrong. It was like being a detective except that solving the mystery meant helping a person get better. But I also know that my ability as a doctor will depend on how well I am educated. I know that for some students going to college is about getting grades and a general education. But for me it's not only about learning but in the future someone's life may depend on how much I learned.

A: To me, education represents a limitless future. At this point in my life, I can be anything. I can be a doctor, teacher, computer programmer or artist. There are a thousand different directions I could go in, but the only way to get there is through education. I am studying English with a minor in music. In my classes, I have done a variety of things from writing a research paper on the role of women writers to composing an original piece performed by my school's orchestra. This is what education is all about. Exploring your interests and discovering what really excites you. So I guess what edu-

Tip #2 From A Scholarship Winner
Brian C. Babcock, U.S. Military Academy

"One of the best things that I did was do a couple of practice interviews. The way we did it was that all of the Truman applicants at my school would meet over lunch with an expert on a topic and talk about it. For example, we'd have someone come in and we'd discuss the 'don't ask don't tell policy.' We were able to get the former drug czar to sit down and talk to us for an hour and a half about the drug policy. Not a bad person to speak with about the drug policy.

"My advice is to go into the interview thinking that you're just going to have a very fun discussion. I didn't have an interview. I had a talk with eight people around the table. They asked me difficult questions but it wasn't hostile."

Brian's contributions reflect his own opinions, not those of the U.S. military.

cation really means to me is the chance to find out who I am by being able to try, succeed and sometimes even fail.

Comments

Both of these answers make personal what could otherwise be a very general answer. Instead of recounting the history of education or statistics from the latest national survey on education, these answers reveal how education has personally affected the students. When you are answering this question ask: What have you personally gained from your education or what do you hope to gain? What benefits have you witnessed from the educational system? Try to be specific. It's not enough to say that you value education. Who doesn't? Try to get at the root cause for why education is important. Give specific examples so that the judges will understand your personal reason for pursuing a degree.

$Q:$ **What has influenced you to get a college education?**

$A:$ I am the first person from my family to attend college. My parents immigrated to the U.S. when I was a child. Without a college education my parents turned to what they knew, which was running a restaurant. I have also had to work in the family restaurant since I was a child so I know how difficult the work is. They said that their dream was for me to go to college so that I would have a wide choice of careers. They don't regret their decision coming to the U.S. because they expect me to go to college and succeed. Attending college means that I will have opportunities that my parents never had and that I will reach not only my goals but the goals of my parents as well. They have sacrificed their lives for me to have a better one. I don't plan on letting them down.

A: Since most of the students from my high school go to college, this seems like a strange question since it was almost assumed by my parents, teachers and friends that college was the next step after graduating. But, I look at going to college as my chance to pursue what I love—which is to design and build robots. I don't know what the job market is for "robot builders" but I intend to find out, and the first step is to get a solid education. I am choosing which schools to apply to based on whether or not they offer classes in robotics. College represents the first step in my ultimate goal of merging what I love to do with a career.

Comments

Both of these answers go beyond what's expected. Almost every-one can say that they want to go to college because they think education is important. What makes these answers strong is that they are specific to the individual. Try to personalize your an-swer by explaining why you have been inspired to get a college degree. What specific incident or person motivated you? What do you hope to gain? Be as specific as possible to give the selec-tion committee insight into what inspires you and to avoid rely-ing on overused generalizations. Also, be sure to stay away from saying that you are going to college just to earn more moolah. On a practical level, earning your degree will enable you to earn more money, but you should focus on less-materialistic factors.

Q: **Why did you choose your college?**

A: When I was researching colleges, I figured out that I had three priorities. First, I wanted a college with a strong program in biology and opportunities for doing hands-on research as an undergraduate. This was important because I plan to become a researcher after graduating and want to get useful experience during my college years. Second, I wanted to attend a school in which classes were taught by professors and not graduate students. I learn best when I am inspired, and I knew that I would be best inspired by learning directly from professors who are shaping the field of biology. My third priority was to attend a school with diversity. I think that college is a place not only for book learning but for personal learning as well. It's my chance to meet people with different ideas and from different backgrounds.

Comments

This is an excellent example of how to reveal something about yourself through your answer. You don't want to be a tour guide, describing the well-known assets of your college. Explain why your college's features are important to you. Instead of saying that you chose your college because of its research facilities, explain how you plan to make use of the facilities. The more details and specifics you can give the better. If appropriate, walk the judges through the thought process you went through when selecting your college. This will help them understand what is important to you and also show them how seriously you consider your college education.

Academic Questions

Q: **What is your favorite subject in school and why?**

A: I enjoy studying English because I like writing. When I write, I feel like I can be myself or I can be a totally different person. I can step into the shoes of someone in the past or be someone who I'm not—like an explorer in the Sahara. Writing lets me see through another person's eyes and forces me to experience what their life must be like. The most difficult thing I ever wrote was a short story about a woman which won an award from my school's literary magazine. The hardest part was not the story but the fact that as a male I had to completely reevaluate how I viewed my world through the eyes of a woman. I can tell you that I have a whole new understanding of what life might be like for the opposite sex.

A: My favorite subject is civics. Most people don't understand the way that our government works and why so many checks and balances have been put into place. It's a system that doesn't always produce the results that I'd like to see, but I am fascinated by our attempts to make a system that is as close to perfect as possible. I can see myself working in government in the future.

Comments

Both of these answers clearly explain the applicants' choices. It would be easy to just name your favorite subject and leave it at that. But the judges are trying to understand why you like what you like. When answering a question like this, give reasons or examples for your selection. Don't state the obvious. If you are asked why English is your favorite subject, give more than "Because I like it" or "Because I'm good at it." You can also use a question like this as an opportunity to talk about an achievement or award. If you say that your favorite subject is English, you can speak about a writing competition that you won or the reading marathon that you started. This is a good springboard question in which you can expand to bring in impressive achievements.

Q: Why did you select your major?

A: I'm majoring in history. What intrigues me about history is the fact that there are so many ways to describe the same event. A good example is the Second World War. There are many different viewpoints depending on which country you were from, whether you were in the military or a civilian or at what level in the lead-

Tip #3 From A Scholarship Winner
Emanuel Pleitez, Stanford University

"Be confident. Confidence is going to help you out in immeasurable ways. Some people think the interviewer is there just to ask questions and make you falter. Usually the interviewers are really nice and they want to get to know you. As long as you let the interviewer know what you're really about, you'll be fine. Smile and let the interviewer get to know you. To do this all you really need is confidence."

ership you were. It's the historian's job to present the information in the most objective way possible while still understanding that there are a lot of subjective elements to history. To me it's like unraveling a mystery, except that the mystery is real.

A: My major is sociology. I hadn't planned to study sociology, but in my first year I took a class on women and the law. In the class we covered the history and effect of laws on women including laws covering maternity leave, pornography and employment. It was an eye-opening class in which we got to interact with women who had been personally affected by these laws. I was hooked. One of my most recent research papers is based on a survey of working-class women. I really care about this field and can relate to it in a personal way.

Comments

Both answers share the applicants' inspiration for selecting their majors. Try to bring the judges into your mind so that they understand why you are passionate about your field. Examples also help the judges, who may have no idea what your major is about, understand why you choose your field. Bring up some interesting facts about your major or hot issues in the field. You might try to also think about how your degree will help you after you graduate. What effect on your future might your choice have? What are your plans for using your degree in the future?

Q: **Which educator has had the most influence on you?**

A: Without a doubt my economics professor. In his lectures he made the theories come to life by showing real life examples of how they worked. He also took the time to meet with each of us individually to get our feedback and to see if we were interested in majoring in economics. My meeting with him lasted for two hours. I explained that I was thinking about majoring in economics but I wasn't sure if I had the mathematical ability. He convinced me that I could work on my math skills as long as I had a passion for learning. I met with him several other times, and he has agreed to be my thesis advisor. Of all my professors, he's the one who has made the most effort to make sure that I was learning and excited about the field.

A: I had a professor last year who taught design. He assigned us projects that I never imagined I'd be doing. At the start of class, he had a handful of toothpicks. He asked us, "What is this?" We all said matter-of-factly, "Toothpicks."

"No," he said. "It's a bridge."

So our assignment was to build a bridge that could support the weight of a bowling ball out of toothpicks. This professor taught me to look at everyday things in a different way, to notice the shape of a gate, the color of the sky after it rained or the shadow of a building on the ground. I learned to pause and appreciate all of the efforts that went into creating what's around me.

Comments

As much as possible try to illustrate the specific influence of your teacher or professor. Give concrete examples of what he or she has done to help you learn. This will give the judges insight into your learning style and what motivates you.

Be sure that you don't just select an educator who was cool, friendly or popular. If you had a teacher or professor with whom you shared a love for baseball but not for the subject matter, this is not a great choice. The judges want to learn about an educator who has inspired you to learn, not one who was a buddy.

Also, don't criticize other educators. In describing your most influential teacher or professor, it is tempting to point out the negative traits of the others. Try not to do this. In many cases, the judges will be educators themselves or will be well-connected with educators. It would be a mistake to insult the profession. Focus on the positive aspects of the educator you choose.

Q: Can you tell me about an academic class, project or other experience that was meaningful for you?

A: One of the most meaningful projects I did was in my English class. We were assigned to develop a plan for the future of our local community. The problem was that the local agriculture industry was deteriorating and within the next five years would leave hundreds in our small community jobless and farm land without a use. We were assigned to create a five-year development plan. We planned the growth of our town, training programs for the displaced workers and redevelopment plans for the land. We each published a report and built a scale model of what the town would look like. Mine was one of the handful selected to be presented at a meeting of our city council.

A: For one of my sociology classes, I had to write a paper based on primary interviews. I knew that in order to be motivated to do the paper I needed to write about something close to me. So I chose to write about the ethnic identities of first- and second-generation Asian American teenagers. Speaking with the teens, I learned how those in the first generation still had close ties to their home country while those in the second generation strived to just fit in with being American. It made me think about my own identity as a third-generation Asian American, and I started to ask questions of my own family. I could see that my family too went through a similar experience. What began as a class assignment actually helped me learn more about my family history.

Comments

This is a great opportunity for you to show off an impressive project. Be sure to give a lot of detail and demonstrate why the project or class was so meaningful. If appropriate, select a subject or project that relates to the scholarship since it will help demonstrate why you deserve to win the award.

Your Career & Future Questions

Q: **Why do you want to enter this career?**

A: I want to be a journalist because I want people to react to my writing. Whether I am uncovering an injustice or celebrating a hero, I want to invoke readers to respond. I recently wrote an article on ethnic barriers on our college's campus and about how students tend to socialize with others of the same ethnic background. That series of articles sparked a huge controversy on campus. The minority clubs asked me to be on a panel discussion on the topic. Over 300 students came. There were a lot of tense moments, but I think they were necessary. My article made people think about a tough subject.

A: It might sound like a cliché to say that I want to become a doctor because of a television show, but for me it's true. I became inspired after watching "ER." I know that the show is a fictionalized drama with the purpose of entertaining and that it is as much about the personal lives of the doctors as the medicine that they practice. But what inspires me is seeing the characters act selflessly for the good of their patients. It's heartening to see that even though people see medical care as impersonal and bureaucratic that these characters give a human and humane face to the field. That's a trait that I think is important and that I want to carry with me when I become a doctor.

Tip #4 From A Scholarship Winner
Dalia Alcázar, U.C. Berkeley

"Sometimes you fill out an application, send it off and it was something you did at 3 a.m. Then you get called in for an interview and you have completely forgotten what you had written.

"Before every interview I made sure I knew about the organization, what I had written on my application and what I had written about for the essay. I needed to know what information they had about me. I also took in resumes and I always carried a portfolio with letters of recommendation, a personal profile, certificates and some examples of my writing."

Comments

When judges ask you this kind of question, what they really want to know is what inspires you. They want to see that you have a reason for entering a profession. Be sure to give a reason even if it is something as simple as being influenced by a TV show. Help the judges understand your inspiration by using lots of examples. They will not only comprehend why you want to work in the industry but also what motivates you in general.

Q: What are your career plans?

A: Eventually I would like to be the managing editor of a major newspaper. I know that I will need to start out working as a journalist for a small circulation paper and slowly move up to higher circulation newspapers. During an internship last summer, I had the opportunity to meet with the managing editor. She described a day in her life and what really struck me was the number of serious decisions she had to make and that every day was different. I don't want to be in a job where I do the same thing every day. I want a job that constantly makes me think and interact with a variety of people. I know it will take years of hard work and perseverance, but I think that I have the decision-making and management ability to do this kind of job well.

A: My goal is to start my own nonprofit organization to provide programs for inner-city youth. In high school and in college I have volunteered with groups to help underprivileged kids. It's been great to see how much of a difference a few hours a week can make in the life of a child. I'm a big sister to a sixth grade student now, and we've developed such a strong relationship that she asked me to go to her sixth grade graduation. I'd begin by working for a nonprofit organization. Eventually I'd like to start my own nonprofit group. I think I can help the most children this way.

Comments

Both of these applicants are aiming high, which is a very good thing. It's important to show the scholarship committee that you have high ambitions, will hold a leadership role in the future and that you are striving to make significant achievements in your career field. Explain how you would like your career to progress and what you would like to achieve. Remember that organizations awarding scholarships have limited funds and want their dollars to have the largest impact possible. This makes it important for scholarship committees to provide their awards to students who will make contributions to the field, who will be role models for others and who may directly participate in their organization in the future. Share with the selection committee what kind of influence you intend to make moving forward. Of course, you don't need to have your entire future planned out. But the scholarship judges do expect that you have a general idea of where you see yourself headed.

Q Where do you see yourself 10 years from now?

A: I've asked myself that very question before and while nothing is set in stone I do have a general idea of what I want to do and where I want to be in a decade. First, I plan to graduate from college with a degree in marketing focusing on marketing communications. After college I'd like to work for a consumer products company to gain practical experience. In 10 years, I'd like to take my big company experience and be a marketing manager at a smaller company, perhaps a start-up. I see myself working in marketing communications because I enjoy writing and I like the challenge of communicating complicated ideas to potential buyers. However, I think ultimately I would enjoy working in a smaller, more intimate environment, which is why I see myself at a smaller company after getting some experience. I also hope to have a family. My career will be important but not as important as my family.

A: I am majoring in political science. In 10 years, I'd like to run a nonprofit organization to help women gain equality in the workplace. Even though there have been gains for women with more serving on executive boards and increasing equity in pay, there is still a long way to go. Through the nonprofit organization, I'd like to provide training and recruitment programs to help women advance in business. I would also like to survey the track records of the representation of women at the executive level and lobby politicians to support women's issues.

A: In 10 years, I hope to be working for a clinic as a pediatrician. I believe that all children have the right to quality medical care whether their parents can afford it or not. Those who have lower incomes do not deserve second-class medical care. That's why I would like to work at a clinic and help the children who need it the most. I would get more personal satisfaction from this than anything else.

Comments

The key to answering this question is acknowledging that the judges want to understand your motivation, not just the fact that you want to be CEO of a company. These students' responses demonstrate their inspiration. Judges also like to see the passion of students who still have their entire future ahead of them. Giving this answer with energy and enthusiasm is essential. Of course, it is possible to go too far and sound naïve. Ideally your answers should be a mix of a healthy dose of youthful idealism with a touch of adult reality.

Activity Questions

Q: **What activities are you involved in?**

For an award for student-athletes:

A: The main activities that I'm involved in are soccer, the academic decathlon and student government. I am the captain of the soccer team, which has won the county championship for the past three years. I plan to continue to play in college. I'm also the co-captain of the academic decathlon team. For the first time in our school's history we've made it to the state level competition, and while it was a team effort, my co-captain and I recruited a teacher to coach us and organized extra study sessions that I think made the difference. For student government, I am the vice president of our school. During my tenure I have directed our school's international festival, canned food drive and election process.

For an award for writing:

A: My most important activity is writing for my school's literary magazine. One piece that I wrote received an award in a writing contest. After traveling to Italy, I decided to write a creative piece about how my life would have been different had my great-grandparents not immigrated to America. I explained what kind of relationship I would have had with my family, my education and my vocation. In my piece, I incorporated memories that my grandparents had of their home country.

Comments

Don't give a laundry list of activities. Instead of telling all 12 clubs that you are a member of, select a handful in which you've made significant contributions. This will be more meaningful to the selection committee and will better capture their attention. Be sure to also highlight activities that match the goal of the awards. If you are applying for a writing award, speak about your writing experience. If you are applying for an award for medicine, speak about your medical-related experience, studies or volunteer work. Make the activities that you describe relevant to the selection committee.

Q: How have you contributed to your community?

A: One of the ways that I have contributed to my community is volunteering over 200 hours at our local library for the children's reading program. Three times a week I go to the library after school to read stories to the children and lead them in arts and crafts activities related to the books. I do this because I think it's important to get kids excited about reading and to expose them to new ideas. The artwork gets them to interact with the material and be creative. I know that the volunteer work that I'm doing is making a difference because parents tell me that their children have learned to enjoy reading more because of my efforts.

A: I have contributed to my community by being a voice for teenagers. Last year there was a series of articles about how teens felt like they were second-class consumers. When we go to a store, we are frequently followed around so that we don't shoplift or we are treated poorly because of our age. I thought that this kind of treatment was unnecessary and wanted to send a message to the stores that were the largest culprits. I organized a protest in front of four of these stores, getting teens to carry picket signs. We got media coverage, and there was another article to follow up on the changes the stores made. We were able to get the owners of all four of the stores to sign pledges to treat teens fairly.

Comments

Show the judges how significant your contribution has been by describing the effects. How many people have you affected? In what way? Have you been honored for your contributions? Contributing to your community can go beyond volunteering. Remember that there are other ways to play a role in your community such as being an advocate for a cause. Your efforts do not have to be part of a formal organization or club.

Opinion Questions

Q: **What is the most important issue to you?**

A: I have been personally affected by underage drinking. A friend of mine was killed in an accident caused by a drunk driver. The accident was devastating not only to her family but also to our entire school. Since that happened, I began volunteering for a group that provides rides for people who have been drinking. Even though the people I drive home are in terrible shape and I ask myself how they could let themselves go so far, I treat them well knowing that at least they had the sense to get a ride home instead of drive themselves. This issue is important to me because I know that my friend's death could have been prevented.

A: It's important to me that children are exposed to the arts. In our school district, funding was cut for the music program at the elementary schools. I volunteered after school to teach students how to play the flute and had 10 students I taught regularly. I believe that the arts encourage students to think creatively, to recognize that there are different ways of communicating and to appreciate the beauty of music. I was exposed to music when I was a child and I think it's important that I help pass on that experience to other children.

Comments

When you are identifying a problem try to also suggest some solutions. It is even more significant if you have tried to be a part of the solution. Of course, you need to be careful not to sound like a Miss America contestant. Don't proclaim that you are going to single-handedly end the world's problems. Be realistic about your role in affecting the issue that you select.

Q: **Is there anything else you want to add?**

A: We spoke about the activities that I'm involved in, but there's an important one that I forgot to mention.

Tip #5 From A Scholarship Winner
Donald H. Matsuda, Jr., Stanford University

"I think the idea with the Truman Scholarship interview is that it's supposed to be somewhat controversial. You go into a room and there is a panel of eight people. They are all distinguished public servants who are trying to test your commitment to your views and get a sense of who you are beyond what you put on paper. You need to be psychologically and emotionally ready for this type of interview so that you won't be surprised."

I've been volunteering at the local art museum as a docent, and the experience has been great. In classes, I've studied modern art. Working at the museum, however, has given me the opportunity to share my appreciation and knowledge with tour groups every week. More than anything else this experience has solidified my desire to become an art curator in the future.

A: I would like to emphasize how committed I am to obtaining my degree and becoming a teacher. I think given the purpose of your award that my background including my work with the after-school program and the awards that I have won for working with children shows that I have fulfilled many of the goals of the award. After graduating, I plan to work as a teacher in my school district. I think it's important that everyone recognizes where they got their start and help others in the same way. That's the only way to make improvements.

Comments

Don't be shy about bringing up something important that the judges didn't ask you about. If you've forgotten to speak about something or a topic never came up during your conversation, now is the time to say so. Use this question to bring up a strong point or two that wasn't discussed. The last impression you leave is often the strongest. If you think you've already left a strong impression, then you don't have to say anything. But if you think you need to reemphasize an important point, then now is the time to make a final statement. Use this opportunity to make sure that you have made it clear why you deserve to win the award.

CHAPTER TEN

JUDGES' ROUNDTABLE:
THE INTERVIEW

In this chapter:

■ Get the inside story from real scholarship judges

■ See what the judges think are the keys to a great interview

■ Learn what mistakes students make in the interview

Meet Your Scholarship Judges

This is the last of three roundtables in this book. In this roundtable, scholarship judges and experts provide insight into the importance of interviews and what you can do to ace them.

If applying for scholarships is like running a race, then the interview is the last lap, the last step toward winning or losing and oftentimes the most important. It is also what worries students the most. Unlike the essay which you can write in the safety of your bedroom, for the interview you actually have to sit across the table from live human beings who are watching and evaluating your every word.

The key to acing the interview is to know what to expect and then to practice. While you may never shed the butterflies in your stomach, you can calm them down. In this roundtable we ask scholarship judges and experts what they are looking for in the interview.

 How important is the interview in determining who wins your award?

Patricia Adams
College Capital
"Most scholarship foundations really enjoy the interview process. After you have narrowed down your applicants, you really want to get a chance to have eye-to-eye contact with the finalists before deciding who wins."

Brent Drage
Rotary International Ambassadorial Scholarship Program
"I would say that the most important part of our process is the interviews. It's important because it allows the Rotarians to speak with the applicants, see what they're like and get an idea of how they would act if they go abroad."

Jacqui Love Marshall
Knight Ridder Minority Scholars Program
"The interview can make a pretty big difference when evaluating two candidates. The interview plays the largest role in the final selection since we use it to narrow down our eight semifinalists to the three finalists."

 # What are some typical questions that you ask?

Because scholarship committees have similar goals–to get to know you beyond your written application and to determine your fit with the award–they ask similar questions. Here are some actual questions you are likely to be asked.

Janet L. Horowitz
Tyco Capital is Pro Education Program
"We provide a sample list of questions to our interviewers to help them generate a dialogue with the interviewee. These include: Do you participate in community activities in your neighborhood? Do you participate in extracurricular activities? What is the one most significant factor that has influenced you to get a college education? How will this scholarship make a difference to you?"

Brent Drage
Rotary International Ambassadorial Scholarship Program
"We typically ask questions related to the autobiographical essay that the student has submitted. We ask applicants to expand on their thoughts and ideas in their essays. We also ask them how they plan on contributing to the world when they graduate. How are they planning on making an impact?"

Jacqui Love Marshall
Knight Ridder Minority Scholars Program
"Typical questions include: Tell me about what you know about the newspaper business. Why do you want to enter into this career? How do your parents feel about your decision to pursue a career in newspapering?"

Q From your experience what are qualities of a good interview?

While there is no single correct way to answer an interview question, there are certain qualities that help to make a good interview stand out in the minds of scholarship judges. It can be difficult to pinpoint what the qualities are, but our panel offers some guidance. Keep in mind that there are a limitless number of ways to have great interviews and these points are meant to provide guidance and a starting point. A good interview does not necessarily need to embody every one of these qualities.

Janet L. Horowitz
Tyco Capital is Pro Education Program
"We like to see applicants who know something about our company. We help by sending them an annual report. If an applicant did not take this opportunity to learn a little about our company it definitely shows through during the interview."

Jacqui Love Marshall
Knight Ridder Minority Scholars Program
"I think being very honest and straightforward is important. We can tell when a student is genuinely interested and passionate about the newspaper business. It is very hard to fake this level of enthusiasm."

Patricia Adams
College Capital
"Something that appeals to many interviewers is when a student has a grateful attitude and is not too cocky. When people are giving away money for free, they want to give it to people who are truly appreciative. Being confident, believing in yourself, your dreams and your goals is one of the most important characteristics to continually work on."

Q What common mistakes do students make in interviews?

Scholarship interviews are one place where it may seem like there's nowhere to hide and every misspoken word is magnified. In most cases, you are probably your harshest critic, noticing your errors more than your interviewers. But we found that there are some mistakes that judges notice more than others. Fortunately, these mistakes are all avoidable.

Janet L. Horowitz
Tyco Capital is Pro Education Program
"Arriving late is a big mistake. You need to remember that we have a tight schedule and are interviewing students back to back. If you show up late it throws off the whole schedule and you certainly don't win any points with us."

Russ Hobbs
Rotary International Ambassadorial Scholarship Program
"Not doing your homework on our organization is an easy mistake to avoid. We had one applicant who attended an Ivy League college and flew across the country for his interview. When the selection committee asked him what he knew about Rotary he didn't have a clue. He relied completely on the fact that he was an Ivy League graduate. It was like applying for a job at IBM without knowing what IBM does. This applicant figured all he had to do was show up and sign for the check."

Patricia Adams
College Capital
"The worst thing you can do is to have a cocky, know-it-all attitude. It's a real turn-off in general but especially in a scholarship interview. You need to have the ability to convince someone that you're worthy of the award. You should always expect the best, but be genuinely appreciative if you win, too."

Leah Carroll
U.C. Berkeley Haas Scholars Program
"When we advise Berkeley students who are about to go into a difficult interview we remind them that they have to see this as intellectual sparring. You need to be prepared for an interviewer

to challenge your ideas. You need to be able to defend your views and even poke back. We tell our students to go in with the attitude that it's challenging but also fun. We have found that a lot of judges are most impressed when students are willing to defend who they are and feel good about their beliefs. Not being ready to do this or not practicing for this kind of interview is a huge mistake."

Q How should students prepare for interviews?

While interviews can be stress-inducing, there is something you can do to combat the tension–prepare. Here is some guidance for getting ready for the main event.

Janet L. Horowitz
Tyco Capital is Pro Education Program
"Role playing. I think students should be doing this with their guidance counselors or anyone who can give them good feedback. Students should also know what the company does, where we're located. It takes two seconds to get a cursory overview of what the company is about and yet it tells a lot about the student who prepares."

Russ Hobbs
Rotary International Ambassadorial Scholarship Program
"There are certain things that you can do to prepare for the interview. The no-brainer is knowing a little bit about Rotary. The interview is not designed to be a test like do you know all the capitals in the U.S. We presuppose that everyone is smart. What we're more interested in is the applicants themselves. What do you believe in? What do you stand for? Those aren't things that you can bone up on. They're either part of who you are or not."

Patricia Adams
College Capital
"I've always said that when you are going for an interview, whether it's for a job, first date or to win a scholarship, it's imperative that you put your best foot forward. That means your manners and clothes have to be impeccable. You should smell

good and have brushed your teeth. If you think it doesn't matter if you wear appropriate shoes, it does matters. Whenever you're trying to make a good impression, everything matters."

Georgina Salguero
Hispanic Heritage Youth Awards
"The interview is your 15 minutes of glory. This is not the time to be modest. You have bragging rights. Use this opportunity. Prepare for it and know what you want to say."

Participating Judges & Experts

Patricia Adams, President and CEO, College Capital

Leah Carroll, Coordinator, U.C. Berkeley Haas Scholars Program and former Program Coordinator, U.C. Berkeley Scholarship Connection

Brent Drage, Resource Development Assistant, Rotary International Ambassadorial Scholarship Program

Russ Hobbs, District Scholarship Chairman, Rotary International Ambassadorial Scholarship Program

Janet L. Horowitz, Assistant Vice President of Corporate Philanthropy, Tyco Capital is Pro Education Program

Jacqui Love Marshall, Vice President of Human Resources, Diversity and Development, Knight Ridder Minority Scholars Program

Georgina Salguero, Senior Manager, Programs and Events, Hispanic Heritage Youth Awards

FINAL THOUGHTS

In this chapter:

- A personal ending

- A special request

A Personal Ending

When you are just beginning your scholarship search it may seem like a daunting–if not downright impossible–task. But you need to keep in mind that the rewards of finding and applying for scholarships are substantial. Every student we interviewed recalled how that when starting it seemed like winning was a long shot. However, each student did apply and ultimately won.

In this book you have met students who have won tens of thousands of dollars in scholarship money. You no doubt have noticed that each has different backgrounds, achievements and aspirations. When you are applying, take the time to highlight your strengths. Show the scholarship judges why you deserve to win.

You can do it. And the fact that you have made your way to the end of this book shows not only your commitment to winning but also gives you a tremendous advantage. Now you know what it takes to write a powerful essay and deliver a knockout interview. You have been witness to success and failure and learned from both.

We wrote this book because we wish that we had known what we do now back when we were applying. Although we were successful, we also learned some hard lessons that we want you to avoid.

We would like to end with a personal story. When I (Kelly) was applying for scholarships I found one offered by my father's company. I was a junior in high school and didn't have any idea what it took to win a scholarship.

I thought that scholarships were based entirely on grades and test scores. Since I had good grades and high PSAT scores I thought I would win. I quickly filled out the application and wrote an essay. When it came time to interview I didn't even practice. I went in cold and "winged it." The whole time I assumed that I would win based on my academic achievements. In fact, I was so confident that I actually spent the rest of the summer waiting for the check to arrive.

But the check never came.

When I found out who won I was shocked. The student had lower grades and test scores than I did! Why did he win? How unfair!

That's when I realized that the scholarship committee was looking for more than good grades and test scores. The following year I spent time on my essay. I also practiced for the interview with a friend.

While I had spent much more time and effort this time I was rewarded when one day, out of the blue, an envelope arrived with a $2,500 check enclosed.

You can win a scholarship through your essay and interview. Even though you might be tempted like I was to bang out an essay and run into an interview cold, don't. You'll spend less time but you won't win.

It takes time and effort to craft a powerful essay and hone your interview skills. But there are a lot of awards out there and someone has to win. Let's make sure that it's you.

Special Request

Before you embark on your own quest for scholarships, we have a special request. We would love to hear about your experiences with scholarships. We want to know what works and what doesn't and how this book has helped you. Please send us a note after you've finished your own money-winning scholarship essays and interviews. You can reach us at:

Gen and Kelly Tanabe
Money-Winning Scholarship Essays and Interviews
c/o SuperCollege
4546 B10 El Camino Real, #281
Los Altos, CA 94022

gen@supercollege.com
kelly@supercollege.com

APPENDIX A SCHOLARSHIP DIRECTORY

This appendix provides additional information about select scholarships included in this book.

Association for Women in Science (AWIS)

Sponsor: AWIS Educational Foundation
Purpose of award: To recognize the achievements of female students in the sciences.
Amount: $1,000.
Eligibility criteria: For the undergraduate program, applicants must be female high school seniors who plan to study the sciences and plan careers in research or teaching. Applicants must be U.S. citizens who plan to attend a college or university in the U.S. and have a minimum 3.75 GPA and a minimum SAT score of 1200 or a minimum ACT composite score of 24. Applicable fields include the behavioral, life and physical sciences and engineering. For the graduate program, applicants must be female students in a behavioral, life, physical or social science or engineering program leading to a Ph.D.
Number of recipients: Varies.
Deadline: January.
For more information or to receive an application:
Association for Women in Science
1200 New York Avenue, Suite 650
Washington, DC 20005
Website: www.awis.org

California Interscholastic Federation (CIF) Scholar-Athlete of the Year

Sponsor: California Interscholastic Federation (CIF)
Purpose of award: To recognize high school student-athletes with exemplary academic and athletic careers and personal standards.
Amount: $2,000 and expense-paid trip to the California State Capitol.
Eligibility criteria: Applicants must be high school seniors with a minimum unweighted GPA of 3.7, demonstrate outstanding athletic performance in a minimum of two years of varsity play in California and exhibit character, trustworthiness, respect, responsibility, fairness, caring and citizenship.
Number of recipients: 2.
Number of applicants: Approximately 1,100.
Deadline: March.

For more information or to receive an application:
CIF State Office
Attn: CIF Scholar-Athlete of the Year
664 Las Gallinas Avenue
San Rafael, CA 94903
Website: www.cifstate.org

Chicago Scholars Award

Sponsor: The Chicago Scholars Foundation
Purpose of award: To recognize high school seniors in the Chicago area who have overcome considerable obstacles to succeed in high school and attend college.
Amount: $1,000.
Eligibility criteria: One award is presented to one senior from each Chicago high school graduating class. Applicants must be nominated by their high school and be Chicago residents or attend a Chicago high school and have a minimum 2.5 GPA. Applicants' financial need is also a consideration.
Number of recipients: Approximately 110.
Deadline: Varies.
For more information or to receive an application:
The Chicago Scholars Foundation
333 West Wacker Drive, 33rd Floor
Chicago, IL 60606
Website: www.chicagoscholars.org

Coca-Cola Scholars Program

Sponsor: Coca-Cola Scholars Foundation
Purpose of award: Begun in 1986 to celebrate the Coca-Cola Centennial, the program is designed to contribute to the nation's future and to assist a wide range of students.
Amount: 50 four-year $20,000 scholarships and 200 four-year $4,000 scholarships.
Eligibility criteria: Applicants must be high school seniors in the U.S. and must use the awards at an accredited U.S. college or university.
Number of recipients: 250.
Deadline: October.

For more information or to receive an application:
Coca-Cola Scholars Foundation
P.O. Box 442
Atlanta, GA 30301-0442
Website: www.coca-cola.com

Discover Card Tribute Award Scholarships

Sponsor: Discover Card in cooperation with the American
Association of School Administrators (AASA)
Purpose of award: To recognize high school juniors for their
accomplishments beyond academics.
Amount: 9 awards of $2,500 in each state. 9 national-level
awards of $25,000.
Eligibility criteria: Applicants must be high school juniors at
an accredited U.S. high school and have a minimum cumula-
tive GPA of 2.75 on a 4.0 scale. Applicants must show accom-
plishments in three of the four following areas: Special Talents,
Leadership, Obstacles Overcome and Community Service.
Number of recipients: Approximately 460.
Number of applicants: Approximately 10,000.
Deadline: January.
For more information or to receive an application:
Discover Card Tribute Award Scholarships
American Association of School Administrators
P.O. Box 9338
Arlington, VA 22219
Website: www.discovercard.com/tribute.htm or www.aasa.org/
discover.htm

Duke University, Angier B. Duke Memorial Scholarship

Sponsor: Duke University
Purpose of award: To recognize intellectually outstanding
students who show promise of being intellectual leaders.
Amount: Full tuition for four years, six-week summer study
program at Oxford, England. The estimated total value of the
award is more than $100,000.
Eligibility criteria: Duke applicants are considered for the
award. The admissions office makes recommendations of
students to the Angier B. Duke Advisory Committee, which
selects the finalists and the winners.

Number of recipients: Approximately 15.
Number of applicants: All Duke applicants are considered for the award.
Deadline: January.
For more information or to receive an application:
Duke University Office of Undergraduate Admissions
2138 Campus Drive
P.O. Box 90586
Durham, NC 27708
Website: www.duke.edu

Fulbright Grants

Sponsor: U.S. Department of State
Purpose of award: According to the State Department's website, the purpose of the program is to "increase mutual understanding between the people of the United States and the people of other countries."
Amount: Varies.
Eligibility criteria: Applicants must be graduate students, scholars or professionals. Refer to the address or website below for complete eligibility criteria.
Number of recipients: Varies.
Deadline: Varies.
For more information or to receive an application:
Office of Academic Exchange Programs
Bureau of Educational and Cultural Affairs
U.S. Department of State, SA-44
301 4th Street, S.W., Room 234
Washington, DC 20547
Website: http://exchanges.state.gov

Hispanic Heritage Youth Awards

Sponsor: Hispanic Heritage Awards Foundation
Purpose of award: To promote Hispanic excellence and recognize the contributions of Hispanic American youth.
Amount: Regional winners receive a $2,000 educational grant, laptop computer and the opportunity to make a $1,000 donation to the charity of their choice. National winners receive an additional $5,000 award and trip to attend the Hispanic Heritage Awards ceremony.

Eligibility criteria: High school seniors who are citizens or permanent residents of the U.S.; who reside in Chicago, Denver, Dallas, Los Angeles, Miami, New York City, Philadelphia, Phoenix, San Antonio, San Diego, San Jose and Washington DC; and who have Hispanic parentage (Hispanic parentage can be one parent of Mexican, Central American, Cuban, Puerto Rican, South American, Spanish or Caribbean Hispanic descent.) Selection criteria include achievement in the applicant's discipline, involvement in community, ability to overcome adversity and character. The disciplines are: Academic Excellence, Sports, the Arts, Literature/Journalism, Mathematics, Leadership/Community Service and Science and Technology.
Number of recipients: 84 regional and 7 national winners.
Deadline: February.
For more information or to receive an application:
Hispanic Heritage Awards Foundation
2600 Virginia Avenue, NW Suite 406
Washington, DC 20037-1905
Website: www.hispanicawards.org

Hispanic Scholarship Fund

Sponsor: Hispanic Scholarship Fund (HSF)
Purpose of award: To strengthen America by advancing the college education of Hispanic Americans. Over the past 25 years, HSF has awarded more than 45,000 scholarships totaling more than $58 million to students who have attended 1,300 colleges and universities.
Amount: Varies.
Eligibility criteria: HSF awards several scholarships including the College Scholarship Program, Community College Transfer Scholarship Program, High School Scholarship Program and Gates Millennium Scholars Program. For the College Scholarship Program, applicants must be of Hispanic heritage (one parent must be fully Hispanic or both parents must be half Hispanic), be U.S. citizens or permanent residents, have earned at least 15 undergraduate college credits in the U.S. or Puerto Rico with a minimum GPA of 2.7 and attend an accredited U.S. college full-time. Selection is based on academic achievement, letter of recommendation, personal statement and financial need. For the High School Scholarship Program,

applicants must be high school seniors with a minimum GPA of 3.0, be U.S. citizens or legal permanent residents of Hispanic background and plan to enroll on a full-time basis in an accredited four-year college or university.

Number of recipients: Varies.
Deadline: October.
For more information or to receive an application:
Hispanic Scholarship Fund
One Sansome Street, Suite 1000
San Francisco, CA 94104
Website: www.hsf.net

Imation Computer Arts Scholarship Program

Sponsor: Imation Corporation
Purpose of award: To promote the use of technology in arts education and encourage innovation among high school students.
Amount: $1,000.
Eligibility criteria: Applicants must attend high school or be home-schooled in the U.S. and must be nominated to the national competition by their schools. Selection is based on quality and creativity of the submitted artwork.
Number of recipients: 25.
Number of applicants: Approximately 500.
Deadline: December.
For more information or to receive an application:
Imation Corporation
Attn.: Community Affairs Manager
1 Imation Place
Oakdale, MN 55128-3414
Website: www.imation.com

Intel Science Talent Search

Sponsor: Intel Corporation and Science Service
Purpose of award: To recognize excellence in science among the nation's youth and encourage the exploration of science.
Amount: Over $1 million awarded each year. 300 semifinalists win $1,000. 30 finalists win $5,000. The top 10 prizes range from $20,000 to $100,000.

Eligibility criteria: Applicants must be high school seniors in the U.S., Puerto Rico, Guam, Virgin Islands, American Samoa, Wake or Midway Islands or the Marianas. Applicants must complete college entrance exams and complete individual research projects and provide a report on the research.
Number of recipients: 300.
Deadline: November.
For more information or to receive an application:
Intel Science Talent Search
Science Service
1719 N Street, NW
Washington, DC 20036
Website: www.intel.com

Johns Hopkins University's Hodson Trust Scholarship

Sponsor: Johns Hopkins University
Purpose of award: To recognize outstanding students who are applying to Johns Hopkins. The Office of Student Financial Services stresses that the main sources of financial aid at Johns Hopkins are need-based. However, merit-based awards account for about 8 percent of all financial aid including athletic scholarships.
Amount: $20,000 per year, renewable for four years.
Eligibility criteria: All applicants are considered for the award.
Number of recipients: Approximately 15 to 20 in each entering freshman class.
For more information or to receive an application:
Johns Hopkins University Undergraduate Admissions
140 Garland Hall
3400 North Charles Street
Baltimore, MD 21218
Website: www.jhu.edu

Knight Ridder Minority Scholars Program

Sponsor: Knight Ridder Inc.
Purpose of award: To support minority students who are interested in pursuing careers in newspapering in either journalism or business.

Amount: $40,000 over four years. Many companies also give their local winners a one-time $500 award.

Eligibility criteria: Students must be graduating high school seniors from communities in which Knight Ridder companies operate. These include the areas surrounding *The Detroit Free Press, The Miami Herald, The Philadelphia Inquirer* and *The San Jose Mercury News*. Recipients commit to work for a Knight Ridder company for four summer internships and for at least one year after graduation.

Number of recipients: Up to 4 business and journalism scholars.

Deadline: Varies by newspaper.

For more information or to receive an application:
Office of Diversity
Knight Ridder
50 West San Fernando Street, Suite 1200
San Jose, CA 95113
Website: www.kri.com

Let's Get Creative Short Story & Poetry Scholarship Contest

Sponsor: FreSch! Free Scholarship Search

Purpose of award: To show appreciation for the visitors to the FreSch! website. Advertising revenue generated from the site is used to fund the scholarship.

Amount: Short stories can win up to $1,000. Poetry can win up to $250.

Eligibility criteria: Applicants must be U.S. citizens or permanent legal residents or Canadian citizens or permanent legal residents. Applicants must also be current high school seniors, college undergraduates or graduate students attending, at least part-time, any accredited college in the U.S. or Canada.

Number of recipients: 3 short story winners and 2 poetry winners.

Deadline: June.

For more information or to apply:
"Let's Get Creative!" Scholarship Entry
779 Denver Avenue
Calhan, CO 80808
Website: www.freschinfo.com

Marshall Scholar

Sponsor: Marshall Aid Commemoration Commission
Purpose of award: Established in 1953 and financed by the British government, the scholarships are designed to bring academically distinguished Americans to study in the United Kingdom to increase understanding and appreciation of the British society and academic values.
Amount: Funding for two or three years of study at a British institution.
Eligibility criteria: Applicants must be U.S. citizens who expect to earn a degree from an accredited four-year college or university in the U.S. with a minimum GPA of 3.7. Students may apply in one of eight regions in the U.S.
Number of recipients: 40.
Deadline: October.
For more information or to receive an application:
Contact your regional center at the address listed on the website.
Website: www.marshallscholarship.org

The Music Center Spotlight Awards

Sponsor: The Music Center
Purpose of award: To identify and reward the outstanding performers of the future.
Amount: Each year, $45,000 in scholarships is awarded to the 12 finalists competing in dance, instrumental music and voice and $15,000 to visual artists through the poster and photography competitions.
Eligibility criteria: Applicants must be performers and visual artists who are currently enrolled in the 9th through 12th grades in any public, private, professional or parochial school. Students must live in one of the following counties: San Diego, Orange, Riverside, San Bernardino, Los Angeles, Ventura or Santa Barbara.
Number of recipients: 12.
Number of applicants: 1,300.
Deadline: Starting in October.
For more information or to receive an application:
The Music Center Spotlight Awards
717 West Temple Street

Los Angeles, CA 90012
Website: www.musiccenter.org

National Honor Society Scholarship

Sponsor: National Honor Society and National Association of Secondary School Principals
Purpose of award: To recognize NHS members.
Amount: $1,000.
Eligibility criteria: Each chapter may nominate two senior members. Nominees must demonstrate character, scholarship, service and leadership.
Number of recipients: 200.
Number of applicants: Approximately 9,000.
Deadline: January.
For more information or to receive an application:
Nomination forms are available from your local NHS chapter adviser.
Website: www.principals.org

National Merit Scholarship Program & National Achievement Scholarship Program

Sponsor: National Merit Scholarship Corporation
Purpose of award: To provide scholarships through a merit-based academic competition.
Amount: Varies.
Eligibility criteria: Applicants must be enrolled full-time in high school, progressing normally toward completion and planning to enter college no later than the fall following completion of high school, be U.S. citizens or permanent legal residents in the process of becoming U.S. citizens and take the PSAT/NMSQT no later than the 11th grade. Participation in the program is based on performance on the exam.
Number of recipients: 50,000. Of these 50,000 students, approximately 34,000 become commended students and approximately 16,000 become semifinalists. Of the semifinalists, approximately 8,000 become finalists.
Number of applicants: 1.2 million students are eligible.
For more information or to receive an application:
National Merit Scholarship Corporation
1560 Sherman Avenue, Suite 200

Evanston, IL 60201-4897
Website: www.nationalmerit.org

Optimist International Essay, Oratorical & Communications Contests

Sponsor: Optimist International
Purpose of award: To reward students based on their essay-writing, oratorical and communications performance.
Amount: Varies.
Eligibility criteria: For the essay contest, applicants must be high school students from North America and must write essays about freedom. For the oratorical contest, applicants must be students in the U.S., Canada or Caribbean under the age of 16. For the communications contest, applicants must be students up to grade 12 in the U.S. and Canada, to CEGEP in Quebec and to grade 13 in the Caribbean who are recognized by their schools as deaf or hard of hearing.
Number of recipients: Varies.
Deadline: February for the essay contest, July for the oratorical contest and September for the communications contest.
For more information or to receive an application: Contact your local Optimist Club.
Website: www.optimist.org

Presbyterian Church USA (PCUSA)

Sponsor: PCUSA
Purpose of award: The Service Programs award provides educational assistance for students who serve their school, church or community. The National Presbyterian College Scholarship recognizes outstanding students.
Amount: $1,500 for the Service Program award. $500 for the College Scholarship.
Eligibility criteria: For the Service Program award, applicants must be in their second or third year of college, have volunteered for a minimum of 250 hours and be recommended by the pastor or chaplain at their school. For the College Scholarship, applicants must be members of the Presbyterian Church, U.S. citizens or permanent residents and high school seniors planning to attend a participating college related to PCUSA.
Number of recipients: Varies.

Deadline: April.
For more information or to receive an application:
Office of Financial Aid for Studies
Presbyterian Church (USA)
100 Witherspoon Street, M042A
Louisville, KY 40202-1396
Website: www.pcusa.org

Principal's Leadership Award

Sponsor: Herff Jones and National Association of Secondary
School Principals (NASSP)
Purpose of award: To recognize students for their leadership.
Amount: $1,000.
Eligibility criteria: Applicants must be nominated by their
high school principal. Each principal can nominate one student
leader from the senior class. Application packets are mailed
each fall to every secondary school.
Number of recipients: 150.
Deadline: December.
For more information or to receive an application:
Check with your high school counselor or principal.
Website: www.principals.org or www.herff-jones.com

Prudential Spirit of Community Award

Sponsor: The Prudential Insurance Company of America and
National Association of Secondary School Principals
Purpose of award: To recognize students for their self-initiated
community service.
Amount: $1,000 for state finalists. National recipients win an
additional $5,000.
Eligibility criteria: Applicants must be middle and high
school students in the U.S. or Puerto Rico. Schools select one
honoree for every 1,000 students.
Deadline: October.
For more information or to receive an application:
The Prudential Insurance Company of America
751 Broad Street
Newark, NJ 07102-3777
Applications are available online.
Website: www.prudential.com/community or www.principals.org

React Take Action Awards

Sponsor: React Magazine and the New World Foundation
Purpose of award: To honor teenagers who have made contributions to their school or community.
Amount: $20,000 for first place, $1,000 for second place and $250 for runner-ups.
Eligibility criteria: Applicants must make significant contributions to their school or community. Many previous winners have either started their own organization or made sizable contributions to existing organizations.
Number of recipients: 5 first place winners, 10 second place winners and 10 runner-ups.
Deadline: Varies.
For more information or to receive an application:
React Take Action Awards c/o JP Kids
989 Market Street, 2nd Floor
San Francisco, CA 94103
Website: www.react.com

Rhodes Scholar

Sponsor: The Rhodes Scholarship Trust
Purpose of award: According to the Rhodes Scholarship Trust website, the purpose is to recognize "qualities of excellence in young people which would contribute to the world's fight."
Amount: Funds two years of study at the University of Oxford including a maintenance allowance, with a possible renewal of one additional year.
Eligibility criteria: Applicants must be U.S. citizens between the ages of 18 and 24. Applicants must also have a bachelor's degree at the time of the award.
Number of recipients: 32.
Deadline: October.
For more information or to receive an application:
Check with your college or download an application from the website.
Website: www.rhodesscholar.org

Rotary International Ambassadorial Scholarship Program

Organization: Rotary International
Purpose of award: To further international understanding and friendly relations among people of different countries.
Amount: Up to $25,000.
Eligibility criteria: Applicants must be citizens of a country in which there are Rotary clubs and have completed at least two years of college-level coursework or equivalent professional experience before starting their scholarship studies. Initial applications are made through local clubs. Students must be proficient in the language of the proposed host country.
Number of recipients: Approximately 1,100.
Deadline: As early as March for club deadlines.
For more information or to receive an application:
Please contact your local Rotary club or visit the website to download an application.
Website: www.rotary.org/foundation/educational/

Sam Walton Community Scholarship

Sponsor: Wal-Mart Foundation
Purpose of award: Scholarship program sponsored by the Wal-Mart Foundation.
Amount: $1,000.
Eligibility criteria: Applicants must be high school seniors. One award is given for each Wal-Mart and Sam's Club store.
Number of recipients: 2,400.
For more information or to receive an application:
Wal-Mart Foundation
Scholarship Program
702 SW 8th Street
Bentonville, AR 72716-8071
Website: www.walmartfoundation.org

Scantron Future Educators of America Scholarship

Sponsor: Scantron
Purpose of award: To encourage talented students to enter careers in teaching.
Amount: $1,000.
Eligibility criteria: Applicants must be high school seniors in California, Florida or Texas planning to major in education with a minimum GPA of 3.0. Applicants must also write an essay.
Number of recipients: 10.
Deadline: January.
For more information or to receive an application:
Scantron Scholarship Competition
c/o Anderson Communications Company Inc.
3 Corporate Plaza, Suite 200
Newport Beach, CA 92660
Website: www.scantron.com/scholarship/

Scripps Howard Top Ten Scholarship

Sponsor: Scripps Howard Foundation
Purpose of award: To recognize the top journalism students in the country.
Amount: $10,000.
Eligibility criteria: Applicants are nominated by their college and must be full-time college students entering their junior or senior year and studying journalism. Selection is based on academic achievement, commitment to a career journalism and essay.
Number of recipients: 10.
Deadline: Varies.
For more information:
Scripps Howard Foundation
P.O. Box 5380
Cincinnati, OH 45201-5380
Website: www.scripps.com

Siemens Westinghouse Science & Technology Competition

Sponsor: Siemens Foundation
Purpose of award: To provide national recognition for science research talent.
Amount: Up to $100,000.
Eligibility criteria: Students must submit research reports either individually or in teams of two or three members.
For more information or to receive an application: Contact the Siemens Foundation through their website.
Website: www.siemens-foundation.org

Silver Knight Award

Sponsor: *The Miami Herald* and *El Herald* newspapers
Purpose of award: To recognize students for their academic achievement and contributions to their school and community.
Amount: $1,500 for winners. $500 for honorable mentions.
Eligibility criteria: Applicants must be high school seniors in Miami-Dade and Broward counties in Florida nominated by their schools.
Number of recipients: 28 winners and 42 honorable mentions.
Deadline: January.
For more information or to receive an application: Contact your guidance counselor.
Website: www.silverknightaward.com

SuperCollege.com Parent & Student Scholarship

Sponsor: SuperCollege.com
Purpose of award: Each year SuperCollege.com uses a portion of the proceeds from the sales of its books to award a scholarship to an outstanding high school or college student and parent of a high school or college student.
Amount: $500 to $1,000.
Eligibility criteria: For the student award: Any high school student or college undergraduate. Applicants must be U.S. citizens or legal residents and may study any major and attend or plan to attend any accredited college or university in the U.S. If selected, you must verify your status as a student and as

a U.S. citizen or legal resident. For the parent award: You must be the parent or guardian of a college-bound high school student or college undergraduate. You must also have assisted your child in applying for college or for financial aid. If selected, you must verify your child's status as a student and as a U.S. citizen or a legal resident. Students and parents apply individually.
For more information or to receive an application: Include a self-addressed and stamped envelope.
SuperCollege.com Scholarship Dept. 1315
4546 B10 El Camino Real, #281
Los Altos, CA 94022
Website: www.supercollege.com

Target All-Around Scholarships for Students

Sponsor: Target Department Stores
Purpose of award: To recognize outstanding community service among students.
Amount: $1,000 to $10,000.
Eligibility criteria: Applicants must be high school seniors, high school graduates or current college students and legal U.S. residents age 24 or under. In addition, applicants must enroll in a full-time undergraduate course of study no later than the fall term of the school year at an accredited two-or four-year college, university or vocational-technical school in the U.S.
Number of recipients: Over 2,000.
Deadline: November.
For more information or to receive an application: Visit the Target website or your nearest Target Department store.
Website: www.target.com

Telluride Association Summer Programs

Sponsor: Telluride Association
Purpose of award: Summer program to provide high school students with a college-level, intellectually enriching experience.
Amount: Full tuition, housing and dining scholarship to attend the program.

Eligibility criteria: Applicants must be high school juniors. The association seeks applicants from a variety of socio-economic backgrounds.
Number of recipients: Varies.
Deadline: Nominations due in December.
For more information or to receive an application:
Telluride Association
217 West Avenue
Ithaca, NY 14850
Website: www.telluride.cornell.edu

Toyota Community Scholars

Sponsor: Toyota
Purpose of award: To recognize students for their academic achievement and community involvement.
Amount: 88 regional winners receive $10,000 and 12 national winners receive $20,000 over four years. The total given is over $1 million.
Eligibility criteria: Applicants must be high school seniors nominated by their high school.
Number of recipients: 100.
Number of applicants: Approximately 12,000.
Deadline: Varies.
For more information or to receive an application:
Contact your guidance counselor.
Website: www.toyota.com

Truman Scholar

Organization: Truman Scholarship Foundation
Purpose of award: To provide college junior leaders who plan to pursue careers in government, non-profits, education or other public service with financial support for graduate study and leadership training.
Amount: $30,000 to be used toward graduate study.
Eligibility criteria: Applicants must attend an accredited U.S. college or university and be nominated by the institution. Students may not apply directly. Applicants must be U.S. citizens or U.S. nationals, complete an application and write a policy recommendation.
Number of recipients: 75 to 80.

Deadline: January.
For more information or to receive an application:
See your school's Truman Faculty Representative or contact the foundation.
Truman Scholarship Foundation
712 Jackson Place, NW
Washington, DC 20006
Website: www.truman.gov

Tyco is Pro Education Program

Organization: Tyco Capital
Purpose of award: To assist urban students in the surrounding Newark, New Jersey, community with financing their higher education.
Amount: 4 students are awarded a renewable scholarship of $2,500 per year for four years plus an internship each summer. 6 students are awarded a $500 savings bond.
Eligibility criteria: Ten high schools in the Newark, New Jersey area submit one candidate. The students must be in the top 10 percent of their class and must have financial need.
Number of recipients: 10.
For more information or to receive an application:
Contact your school's guidance counselor.
Website: www.tyco.com

United Negro College Fund Scholarships

Sponsor: United Negro College Fund (UNCF)
Purpose of award: To enhance the quality of education by providing financial assistance to deserving students.
Amount: Varies.
Eligibility criteria: The UNCF general scholarship eligibility criteria are: Students must have a minimum GPA of 2.5 on a 4.0 scale and must have unmet financial need as verified by the Financial Aid Director. Students must also complete a Financial Aid Form (FAF) or a Family Financial Aid Statement (FFS) and request that the Student Aid Report (SAR) be sent to the financial aid office at their college or university.
Deadline: Varies.

For more information or to receive an application:
United Negro College Fund
8260 Willow Oaks Corporate Drive
Fairfax, VA 22031
Website: www.uncf.org

University of Chicago College Honor Scholarship

Sponsor: University of Chicago
Purpose of award: To recognize academically talented high school students.
Amount: Full tuition, renewable for all four years.
Eligibility criteria: All applicants for admission to the university are automatically judged for the scholarship.
Number of recipients: 30 to 35.
Deadline: January.
For more information or to receive an application:
Office of College Admissions
The University of Chicago
1116 E. 59th Street
Chicago, IL 60637
Website: www.uchicago.edu

USA Funds Access to Education Scholarships

Sponsor: USA Funds
Purpose of award: To assist students in achieving their higher education goals.
Amount: The full-time student award is up to $1,500 per year, and the half-time student award is up to $750 per year. Awards may be renewed annually for up to three years, until the student receives a degree or certificate or until the total award reaches $6,000, whichever comes first. Up to $3 million in new scholarships are awarded each year.
Eligibility criteria: This is a need-based scholarship program with aid for full-time and half-time students. Applicants must be high school seniors or other individuals who plan to enroll or are enrolled in full- or half-time undergraduate or graduate coursework at an accredited two- or four-year college, university or vocational or technical school. Students must be U.S. citizens or eligible non-citizens. Applicants must have an annual adjusted gross family income of $35,000 or less. Selec-

tion will also be based on past academic performance and future potential, leadership, participation in school and community activities, work experience and career and educational aspirations and goals. Up to half of the awards are given to members of ethnic minority groups or students who have a documented physical disability. Up to half of the awards are given to applicants in states that USA Funds serves as the designated student loan guarantor: Arizona, Hawaii and the Pacific Islands, Indiana, Kansas, Maryland, Mississippi, Nevada and Wyoming.

Number of recipients: Depends on the mix of full-time and half-time awards.
Number of applicants: Approximately 6,000 per year.
Deadline: April.
For more information or to receive an application:
Call 800-537-4180 or visit the website.
Website: www.usafunds.org

USA Today All-USA Academic Teams

Sponsor: *USA Today*
Purpose of award: To recognize students who excel not only in scholarship but also in leadership roles on and off campus.
Amount: $2,500 for members of the first team.
Eligibility criteria: Full-time undergraduates at four-year institutions in the U.S. and its territories are eligible for the college team. Community and junior college students in the U.S. and its territories are eligible for the two-year college team. Students graduating from a high school in the U.S. and its territories are eligible for the high school team. U.S. citizenship is not required. Special consideration is paid to students' original academic or intellectual product.
Number of recipients: For each category, 20 students are selected for the first team and 40 students are selected for the second and third team.
Deadline: Starting in November.
For more information or to receive an application:
Visit the website to download the nomination form.
Website: http://allstars.usatoday.com

Wendy's High School Heisman Award

Sponsor: Wendy's Restaurants
Purpose of award: To recognize scholarship, citizenship and athletic ability.
Amount: Varies.
Eligibility criteria: Applicants must be high school juniors nominated by their schools.
Number of recipients: 1,200 state finalists, 102 state winners, 12 national finalists.
Deadline: September.
For more information or to receive an application: Contact your high school guidance department.
Website: www.principals.org

APPENDIX B
WEB RESOURCES

This appendix provides online resources to help you find funds to pay for college.

SuperCollege.com

4546 B10 El Camino Real #281
Los Altos, CA 94022
Phone: 650-618-2221
Email: supercollege@supercollege.com
Website: www.supercollege.com
Our publishing company, which focuses on helping students
get into and pay for college. Visit our website to search a free
database of thousands of scholarships, get more financial aid
and scholarship tips and strategies and enter our SuperCollege
student and parent scholarships.

Access America for Students

400 Maryland Avenue, SW
ROB-3, ROOM 4004
Washington, DC 20202-5132
Website: www.students.gov
From the U.S. Department of Education, a directory of govern-
ment websites for planning and paying for your education.
Also contains resources for finding a job, registering for the
Selective Service and applying to be a Peace Corps volunteer.

America's Learning Exchange

Phone: 877-348-0502
Website: www.alx.org
Resources for career exploration, career tools, career testing
and assessment and work-study programs.

CNS—Corporation for National Service

1201 New York Avenue, NW
Washington, DC 20525
Phone: 800-942-2677
Website: www.cns.gov or www.americorps.org
Public service resources including information on AmeriCorps,
a federal program in which you can volunteer for one year and
receive a modest living allowance, health insurance, student
loan deferment, training and a $4,725 education award to help
pay for college, grad school, vocational training or to pay off
student loans. If you serve part-time, you'll get a portion of
that amount.

College Board

Website: www.collegeboard.org
The makers of the SAT and PSAT offer financial aid calculators, a scholarship search and articles on financial aid.

College Capital

Website: www.collegecapital.com
A subscription-based site where you can search for scholarships and colleges. Includes a large database of scholarships, colleges and internships and informational articles on college planning and beyond.

IRS

Phone: 800-829-1040
Website: www.irs.gov
Information on higher-education income tax credits and tax implications of financial aid awards.

National Association of Intercollegiate Athletics

23500 W. 105th Street
P.O. Box 1325
Olathe, KS 66051-1325
Phone: 913-791-0044
Website: www.naia.org
Information on eligibility requirements and financial aid for student-athletes.

National Collegiate Athletic Association (NCAA)

1 NCAA Plaza
700 W. Washington Street
Indianapolis, IN 46204
Phone: 317-917-6222
Website: www.ncaa.org
Information on eligibility requirements and a directory of schools that award scholarships for athletics.

National Junior College Athletic Association

P.O. Box 7305
Colorado Springs, CO 80933-7305

Phone: 719-590-9788
Website: www.njcaa.org
Information on scholarships and awards for student-athletes and individuals based on performance, service, merit and achievement.

National Small College Athletic Association

113 East Bow Street
Franklin, NH 03235
Website: www.thenscaa.com
Information for student-athletes and directory of member schools that award financial aid for athletics.

U.S. Department of Education & Federal Financial Aid

Federal Student Aid Information Center
P.O. Box 84
Washington, DC 20044-0084
Phone: 800-4-FED-AID, TTY 800-730-8913
Website: www.ed.gov
Includes information on completing the FAFSA, federal aid program eligibility, descriptions and deadlines, tips on reducing costs, tax cuts for education and online versions of two informative guides.

Veteran Benefits

Phone: 888-GI-BILL-1 (888-442-4551)
Website: www.gibill.va.gov
Information on educational programs for veterans and their dependents.

Wiredscholar.com

Website: www.wiredscholar.com
Comprehensive financial aid and scholarship website that includes a free scholarship database and informational articles, financial aid calculators and loan information. Wiredscholar also has a set of interactive tools that enable you to analyze the affordability of schools and compare financial aid award letters.

INDEX

A

A Fight Against Discrimination 112–113
A Lesson For Both Of Us 101–102
A Mother's Sacrifice 76–77
Accepted! 50 Successful College Admission Essays 16, 254
Access America for Students 240
accomplishments 56, 114–118, 176–179
Adams, Patricia 204, 206, 207, 208–209
Alcázar, Dalia 85, 195
American Association of School Administrators 39, 153
America's Learning Exchange 240
Angier B. Duke Memorial Scholarship 117, 218–219
Association for Women in Science Scholarship 101, 216
Avian Veterinarian 108–109

B

Babcock, Brian C. 65–66, 170–171, 187
Bagby, Gregory J. 118
Bazemore, Trisha 34, 37, 127, 153
Bei, Sara 85, 120–121
Bengali, Shashank 90–93
Bloom, Jonathan 114–115
Briggs, Tracey Wong 31, 33, 35, 37, 40, 155

C

Camp ReCreation 100–101
Carroll, Leah 75, 155, 170–171, 207–208
Carroll, Wanda 32, 35, 38, 40, 154, 155
Chicago Scholars Award 81, 217
Chiu, Jennifer 73–75
choosing an essay topic 53

CIF Scholar-Athlete of the Year 31, 120, 216–217
Coca-Cola Scholars Program 34, 37, 59, 68, 127, 153, 217–218
Cohen Foundation 76
College Board 241
College Capital 204, 206, 207, 208–209, 241
conclusions for essays 60–61
Corporation for National Service 240
Cryptography And Encryption 114–115

D

Darne, Michael 27, 156
De Anda, Mario A. 40, 155
Deshmukh, Swati 112–113
DiFiore, Laura 33, 36, 38, 41, 51, 154, 155
Discover Card Tribute Award Scholarship 17, 31, 37, 98, 112–113, 116, 218
Dow Scholarship 110
Drage, Brent 23, 31, 39–40, 204, 205

E

Eadie, Mark R. 59, 68–71
editors 58–59, 61
Educationality 137
Edwards, Cathy 31, 37
11-Year-Old Scientist 116–117
essay examples 64–127
  A Fight Against Discrimination 112–113
  A Lesson For Both Of Us 101–102
  A Mother's Sacrifice 76–77
  about academic accomplishments 114–118
  about artistic talents 122–124
  about athletics 120–121

about career plans or field of study 103–111
about community service and volunteerism 97–102
about experiences and challenges 65–75
about family 76–83
about leadership 112–113
about national or international issues 84–96
Avian Veterinarian 108–109
Camp ReCreation 100–101
Cryptography And Encryption 114–115
disasters 130–150
Educationality 137
11-Year-Old Scientist 116–117
Getting Katie Into College 125–126
Giving Back To My Community 98–100
I Love My Family 139–141
Inspired To Teach 67–68
Inspiring Greatness 120–121
International Journalism 103–105
Invisible Handicap 68–71
It's Not My Fault 146–148
Lessons From A Pitbull 73–75
Lessons From The Outdoors 65–66
Liza 144–146
Media Misunderstandings 91–93
My Dedication To The World 133–135
My Family's Hope 82–83
My Name Is Brooke 138–139
My So-Called Life 132–133
My Trip To Europe 135–136
Nuclear Nightmare 148–150
Only The Strong Survive 71–73
Organ Donor Project 94–96
Science Nerd 117–119
Scientific Inspiration 110–111
Serving And Protecting 97–98

STARS 87–88
Ten Years From Now 143–144
Thank You, Dr. Seuss 78–80
The Highway Of Life 141–143
The Power To Change The World 88–90
The Right Fit 106–107
Tokai Nuclear Disaster 84–86
Turningpoint 122–123
When Drinking Water 80–81
Where Has Time Gone? 130–132
essay mistakes 130–150, 154–156
    creativity overload 141–143
    excuses 146–148
    influential person 139–141
    Judges' Roundtable 154–156
    Miss America essay 133–135
    no connection to life 144–146
    no point 130–132
    simple solution 148–150
    sob story 56, 132–133
    too many statistics 138–139
    travel 135–136
    vocabulary 137
    your future 143–144
essays 46–61
    accomplishments 56
    answering the underlying question 50–52
    choosing a topic 53
    conclusions 60–61
    editors 58–59, 61
    examples 64–127
    fit with application 47–49
    importance of 14, 46, 152
    importance of being positive 47, 58
    importance of originality 49–50, 53–54
    importance of passion 52
    introductions 60
    Judges' Roundtable 152–157
    mistakes 51, 130–150, 154–156

qualities of winning essays 49–52, 152–154
recycling 59
research 55
sob stories 56–58
thesis 54–56
using examples 59
writing tips 53–58

F

finding scholarships 20–27
  activities 22
  community and religious organizations 22–23
  counselor or financial aid officer 21
  employer 22
  Internet 20–21
  local businesses 24
  local government 23–24
  newspaper 24
  parents 22–23
  professional organizations 22
  scholarship directories 20
Fortson, Danny 103–105
FreSch! Let's Get Creative Short Story and Poetry Contest 33, 36, 38, 41, 51, 154, 155, 223
Frishberg, Ellen 31, 41
Fulbright Grant 122, 219

G

Get Free Cash For College 16, 20, 252
Get Into Any College 16, 253
Getting Katie Into College 125–126
Giving Back To My Community 98–100
grades, importance of 17

H

Hall, Kimberly 34, 40, 47, 152, 153, 154

Haskins, Jessica 77–80, 85
Heikamp, Emily 117–119
Heras, Daniel 67–68
Hispanic Heritage Youth Awards 30, 33, 37, 153, 156, 209, 219–220
Hispanic Scholarship Fund 40, 155, 220–221
Hobbs, Russ 23, 33–34, 38, 41, 167, 207, 208
Hollenbeck, Eddie 124
Horowitz, Janet L. 21, 35, 36–37, 39, 57, 205, 206 207, 208
Hyde, Lindsay 93–96

I

I Love My Family 139–141
Imation Computer Arts Scholarship 32, 35, 39, 124, 221
Inspired To Teach 67–68
Inspiring Greatness 120–121
Intel Science Talent Search 221–222
International Journalism 103–105
Internet
  finding scholarships 20–21
  guide 239–242
  SuperCollege.com 213, 255
interview examples 176–202
  achievement 176–177
  activities 198–199
  career plans 194–196
  community involvement 199
  education 186–188, 189–190, 192–194
  favorite book 183–184
  future plans 196–197
  issues 200
  leadership 178–179
  major selection 190–191
  reasons for choosing college 189
  role model 181–183

significance of winning 185–186

strengths and weaknesses 179–181

why deserve to win 184–185

interviews 160–173

  asking questions 164

  body language 165–167

  by telephone 169–171, 173

  creating conversation 161–164

  disasters 171–172

  dress 165–167

  examples 176-202

  good qualities of 206

  group 165, 173

  hostile 170–171

  importance of 14, 204–205

  Judges' Roundtable 204-209

  mistakes 207–208

  practicing 168–169

  preparation 162–164, 208–209

  typical questions 205

introductions for essays 60

Invisible Handicap 68–71

IRS 241

Ishida, Marie M. 31

It's Not My Fault 146–148

J

Javaras, Kristin N. 61, 119, 163

Johns Hopkins University Hodson Trust Scholarship 31, 41, 222

Juárez, Elisa Tatiana 86–90, 141, 179, 181

judges

  advice 40–41

  interpreting 181

  interviewing 167

  who they are 32–34

Judges' Roundtable

  essays 152–157

  interviews 204–209

  selection process 30–44

K

Keller, Shirley Kennedy 17, 39, 153

Kendall, Emily 101–102

Kennedy, Chris 107–109

Knight Ridder Minority Scholars Program 25, 32, 33, 37, 55, 71, 105, 152, 153–154, 205, 206, 222–223

Koehler, Andrew 122–123

Kovacs, Patricia R. 32, 35, 39

L

Lee, Nhia TongChai 71–73

Lessons From A Pitbull 73–75

Lessons From The Outdoors 65–66

Liza 144–146

M

Marshall, Jacqui Love 25, 32, 33, 37, 55, 152, 153–154, 205, 206

Marshall Scholar 224

Matsuda, Donald H. 80–81, 85, 96, 100–101, 170–171, 201

Media Misunderstandings 91–93

Michaels, Maggy 125–126

mission of scholarships 26–27, 30–32, 162

Moreno, Corisa 32, 34–35, 38, 39

Morimoto, Jason 85, 119, 173

Murray, Bob 32, 36

Music Center Spotlight Awards 32, 34–35, 38, 39, 224–225

My Dedication To The World 133–135

My Family's Hope 82–83

My Name Is Brooke 138–139

My So-Called Life 132–133

My Trip To Europe 135–136

N

National Association of
    Intercollegiate Athletics 241
National Association of Secondary
    School Principals 32, 36, 38,
    40, 154, 155
National Collegiate Athletic
    Association 241
National Honor Society
    Scholarships 38, 225
National Junior College Athletic
    Association 241–242
National Merit Scholarship
    107, 114, 225–226
National Small College Athletic
    Association 242
Nuclear Nightmare 148–150

O

Oleck, Cecilia A. 105–107
Only The Strong Survive 71–73
Optimist International Essay
    Contest 84, 226
Organ Donor Project 94–96

P

past winners, importance of 27–28
Perplies, Vanessa Deanne 97–98
Pleitez, Emanuel 69, 141, 191
Presbyterian Church USA
    Scholarship 88, 226–227
Principal's Leadership Award
    32, 38, 227
Prudential Spirit of Community
    Award 32, 227

Q

Quezada, Zeke 67

R

React Take Action Award 93, 228
recycling essays 59

Rhodes Scholarship
    61, 119, 163, 228
Roshto, Deborah 111
Rotary International Ambassado-
    rial Scholarships 23, 31, 33–
    34, 38, 39–40, 41, 103
    167, 204, 205, 207, 208, 229

S

Salguero, Georgina
    30, 33, 37, 153, 156, 209
Sam Walton Community Scholar-
    ship 229
SAT, importance of 17
Scantron Scholarship 67, 230
scholarship directories 20
scholarships
    Angier B. Duke Memorial 117,
    218–219
    Association for Women in
    Science 101, 216
    Chicago Scholars Award 81,
    217
    CIF Scholar-Athlete of the
    Year 31, 120, 216–217
    Coca-Cola Scholars Program
    34, 37, 59, 68, 127, 153, 217–
    218
    Cohen Foundation 76
    Discover Card Tribute Award
    17, 31, 37, 98, 112, 116, 218
    Dow 110
    FreSch! Let's Get Creative
    Short Story and Poetry Contest
    33, 36, 38, 41, 51, 154, 155,
    223
    Fulbright Grant 122, 219
    Hispanic Heritage Youth
    Awards 30, 33, 37, 153,
    156, 209, 219–220
    Hispanic Scholarship Fund
    40, 155, 220–221
    Imation Computer Arts
    32, 35, 39, 124, 221

Intel Science Talent Search 221–222

Johns Hopkins University Hodson Trust 31, 41, 222

Knight Ridder Minority Scholars Program 25, 32, 33, 37, 55, 71, 105, 152, 153–154, 205, 206, 222–223

Marshall Scholar 224

Music Center Spotlight Awards 32, 34–35, 38, 39, 224-225

National Honor Society 38, 225

National Merit 107, 114, 225–226

Optimist International Essay Contest 84, 226

Presbyterian Church USA 88, 226–227

Principal's Leadership Award 32, 38, 227

Prudential Spirit of Community Award 32, 227

React Take Action Award 93, 228

Rhodes 61, 119, 163, 228

Rotary International Ambassadorial 23, 31, 33–34, 38, 39–40, 41, 103, 167, 204, 205, 207, 208, 229

Sam Walton Community 229

Scantron 67, 230

Scripps Howard College Journalism 90, 230

Siemens Westinghouse Science and Technology Competition 231

Silver Knight 181, 231

SuperCollege.com 18, 77, 125, 231–232, 240, 255

Target All-Around Scholarships 86, 97, 232

Telluride Association Summer Program 73, 232–233

Toyota Community Scholars 93, 233

Truman 65, 80, 100, 170–171, 201, 233–234

Tyco Capital is Pro Education 21, 35, 36–37, 39, 57, 205, 206, 207, 208, 234

United Negro College Fund 34, 40, 47, 152, 153, 154, 234–235

University of Chicago College Honor Scholarships 235

USA Funds Access to Education 32, 36, 235–236

USA Today All-USA Academic Teams 31, 33, 35, 37, 40, 155, 236

Wendy's High School Heisman Award 32, 237

Science Nerd 117–119

Scientific Inspiration 110–111

Scripps Howard College Journalism Scholarship 90, 230

selecting scholarships 24–26

Serving And Protecting 97–98

Setters, Andrea 110–111

Siemens Westinghouse Science and Technology Competition 231

Silver Knight Scholarship 181, 231

Singla, Svati 98–100, 116–117

Sok, Chheng 81–83

Special Features

   A scholarship support network 69

   Advice from a Rhodes Scholar 163

   Ambassadors wanted 23

   An essay pop quiz 57

   Be true 141

   Essay advice from the winners 85, 119

Essays get better with each revision 61
Focus on solutions 47
Hard to believe but true essay mistakes 51
Looking to make an impact 21
Make sure you make your point 173
Misinterpreting the judges 181
Not just looking for straight "A" students 17
Seeking genuineness 127
The group interview 165
The hostile interview 170–171
The importance of getting editors 96
The importance of going beyond the superficial 55
The intangible benefits of applying 75
Tips from scholarship winners 179, 187, 191, 195, 201
Use examples and illustrate 59
What it's like to be an interviewer 167
When and where to find scholarships 27
Work experience and financial aid 25
STARS 87–88
SuperCollege.com 213, 255
SuperCollege.com Scholarship 18, 77, 125, 231–232, 240, 255

T

Tanabe, Gen S. and Kelly Y. 16, 212–213, 256
Target All-Around Scholarship 86, 97, 232
Telluride Association Summer Program Scholarship 73, 232–233
Ten Years From Now 143–144
Thank You, Dr. Seuss 78–80

The Highway Of Life 141–143
The Power To Change The World 88–90
The Right Fit 106–107
Tokai Nuclear Disaster 84–86
Toyota Community Scholars 94, 233
Truman Scholarship 65, 80, 100, 170–171, 201, 233–234
Turningpoint 122–123
Tyco Capital is Pro Education 21, 35, 36–37, 39, 57, 205, 206, 207, 208, 234

U

U.C. Berkeley Haas Scholars 75, 155, 170, 207
United Negro College Fund 34, 40, 47, 152, 153, 154, 234–235
University of Chicago College Honors Scholarships 235
U.S. Department of Education 242
USA Funds Access to Education Scholarships 32, 36, 235–236
USA Today All-USA Academic Teams 31, 33, 35, 37, 40, 155, 236

V

Valadez, Rodolfo 76–77
veterans' benefits 242

W

Wendy's High School Heisman Award 32, 237
When Drinking Water 80–81
Where Has Time Gone? 130–132
Wiredscholar 27, 156, 242
Wood, Elizabeth Ashlea 84, 86
writing tips for essays 46–61, 130–150, 152–157

MORE GREAT BOOKS & RESOURCES

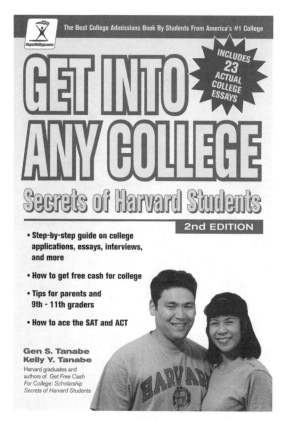

Learn how to get into the college of your dreams

- A complete, step-by-step guide to college admissions
- The secrets of creating a stunning application
- 23 actual college essays that worked
- Tips for parents and 9th to 11th graders
- Lessons from true-life successes and failures of real students
- How to craft an irresistible admission essay
- How to master the interview
- How to ace the SAT and ACT

Get your copy at bookstores or:
Call toll-free 888-264-7108 or visit www.supercollege.com

Get Into Any College (2nd edition)
ISBN: 0-9657556-5-7
Pages: 288
Price: $16.95

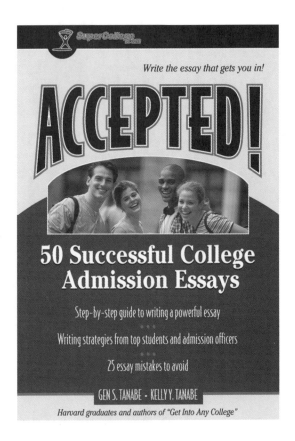

Attention Students & Parents:
Win The SuperCollege.com Scholarships

For students: We reward high school and college undergraduates who excel in both academics and extracurriculars.

For parents: We offer the only scholarship for parents who help support their children with college admission or financial aid.

These scholarships are a part of the ongoing mission of SuperCollege.com to help students get into and pay for the college of their dreams. To apply, visit **www.supercollege.com** where you can download the application. Good luck!

We invite you to visit our website at **www.supercollege.com.** Why? Just look at what you'll find:

- Apply for the SuperCollege.com Scholarships, the only scholarships for both students and parents.
- Search for scholarships that match your background in our free database of thousands of awards.
- Learn more tips and strategies on financial aid, scholarships and college admission.
- Use the SuperCollege MatchMaker to find colleges that fit you.
- Connect with other students who understand what you are going through and can offer helpful advice.
- Parents: Get advice on how you can help your child get into and pay for any college.
- Ask us your most pressing questions.

Visit us at www.supercollege.com for free resources on scholarships, financial aid and college admission.

About The Authors

Harvard graduates Gen S. Tanabe and Kelly Y. Tanabe are the founders of SuperCollege and the award-winning authors of the books *Get Free Cash For College, Get Into Any College* and *Accepted! 50 Successful College Admission Essays.*

Together, Gen and Kelly were accepted to every school to which they applied, all of the Ivy League colleges, and won over $100,000 in merit-based scholarships. They were able to leave Harvard debt-free and their parents guilt-free.

Gen and Kelly give workshops at high schools across the country and write the nationally syndicated "Ask The SuperCollege.com Experts" column. They have made dozens of appearances on television and radio and have served as expert sources for respected publications including *U.S. News & World Report, USA Today*, the *New York Daily News*, the *San Jose Mercury News*, the *Chronicle of Higher Education*, the *Richmond Times Dispatch* and *Rolling Stone.*

Gen grew up in Waialua, Hawaii. Between eating banana-flavored shave ice and basking in the sun, he was president of the Student Council, captain of the Speech Team and a member of the tennis team. A graduate of Waialua High School, he was the first student from his school to be accepted at Harvard. In college, Gen was chair of the Eliot House Committee and graduated *magna cum laude* with a degree in both History and East Asian Studies.

Kelly attended Whitney High School, a nationally ranked public high school in her hometown of Cerritos, California. She was the editor of the school newspaper, assistant editor of the yearbook and founder of a public service club to promote literacy. In college, she was the co-director of the HAND public service program and the brave co-leader of a Brownie Troop. She graduated *magna cum laude* with a degree in Sociology.

Gen, Kelly and their dog Sushi live in Palo Alto, California.